Alberta Police APCAT Study Guide

Alberta Police
Cognitive Ability Test
(APCAT) Study Guide &
Practice Test Questions

COMPLETE
TEST PREPARATION INC.
WWW.TEST-PREPARATION.CA

Copyright © 2025 by Complete Test Preparation Inc. ALL RIGHTS RESERVED. No part of this book may be reproduced or transferred in any form or by any means, graphic, electronic, or mechanical, including photocopying, recording, web distribution, taping, or by any information storage retrieval system, without the written permission of the author.

Notice: Complete Test Preparation Inc. makes every reasonable effort to obtain from reliable sources accurate, complete, and timely information about the tests covered in this book. Nevertheless, changes can be made in the tests or the administration of the tests at any time and Complete Test Preparation Inc. makes no representation or warranty, either expressed or implied as to the accuracy, timeliness, or completeness of the information contained in this book. Complete Test Preparation Inc. makes no representations or warranties of any kind, express or implied, about the completeness, accuracy, reliability, suitability or availability with respect to the information contained in this document for any purpose. Any reliance you place on such information is therefore strictly at your own risk.

The author(s) shall not be liable for any loss incurred as a consequence of the use and application, directly or indirectly, of any information presented in this work. Sold with the understanding, the author(s) is not engaged in rendering professional services or advice. If advice or expert assistance is required, the services of a competent professional should be sought.

The company, product and service names used in this publication are for identification purposes only. All trademarks and registered trademarks are the property of their respective owners. Complete Test Preparation Inc. is not affiliated with any educational institution.

Complete Test Preparation Inc. is not affiliated with the Alberta Police Service, who are not involved in the production of, and do not endorse this publication.

We strongly recommend that students check with exam providers for up-to-date information regarding test content.

Version 9 March 2025

Published by
Complete Test Preparation Inc.
Victoria BC Canada
Visit us on the web at https://www.test-preparation.ca
Printed in the USA

ISBN-13: 9781772454659

About Complete Test Preparation Inc.

Why Us?
The Complete Test Preparation Team has been publishing high quality study materials since 2005, with a catalog of over 145 titles, in English, French and Chinese, as well as ESL curriculum for all levels.

To keep up with the industry changes, we update everything all the time!

And the best part?
With every purchase, you're helping people all over the world improve themselves and their education. So thank you in advance for supporting this mission with us! Together, we are truly making a difference in the lives of those often forgotten by the system.

Charities that we support
https://www.test-preparation.ca/charities-and-non-profits/

You have definitely come to the right place.
If you want to spend your valuable study time where it will help you the most - we've got you covered today and tomorrow.

https://www.test-preparation.ca

Feedback

We welcome your feedback. Email us at feedback@test-preparation.ca with your comments and suggestions. We carefully review all suggestions and often incorporate reader suggestions into upcoming versions. As a Print on Demand Publisher, we update our products frequently.

CONTENTS

6   **Getting Started**
- How this study guide is organized   7
- The APCAT Study Plan   8
- Making a Study Schedule   11

15   **Professional Judgment**
- Self-Assessment   17
- Answer Key   20
- How to Answer this type of Question   21

22   **Recognition and Identification**
- Self-Assessment   23
- Answer Key   25
- How to Answer this type of Question   25

28   **Alberta Communications Test - ACT**
- ACT Self-Assessment   29
- Answer Key   38
- ACT Tutorials   41
- Capitalization   41
- Colons and Semicolons   43
- Commas   44
- Quotation Marks   47
- Common English Usage Mistakes   49
- Subject Verb Agreement   56

63   **Mathematics**
- Self-Assessment   67
- Answer Key   70
- Basic Math Video Tutorials   71
- Fraction Tips, Tricks and Shortcuts   71
- Converting Fractions to Decimals   73
- Decimal Tips, Tricks and Short-cuts   76
- Percent Tips, Tricks and Shortcuts   77
- Types of Word Problems   84

93	**Logic**	
	Logic Self-Assessment	94
	Answer Key	101
	Number Series Tutorial	103
	Types of Number Series	103
	Strategy for Answering	106
107	**Practice Test Questions Set 1**	
	Answer Key	140
150	**Practice Test Questions Set 2**	
	Answer Key	181
191	**After Taking a Practice Test**	
	after you take a practice test	191
	Getting the Most from Practice	192
193	**Conclusion**	
194	**Online Resources**	

Getting Started

CONGRATULATIONS! By deciding to take the Alberta Police Aptitude Test, you have taken the first step toward a great future! Of course, there is no point in taking this important examination unless you intend to do your best to earn the highest grade you possibly can. That means getting yourself organized and discovering the best approaches, methods and strategies to master the material. Yes, that will require real effort and dedication, but if you are willing to focus your energy and devote the study time necessary, before you know it you will be on your way to a brighter future!

We know that taking on a new endeavour can be scary, and it is easy to feel unsure of where to begin. That's where we come in. This study guide is designed to help you improve your test-taking skills, show you a few tricks of the trade

and increase both your competency and confidence.

The Alberta Police Aptitude Test

The APCAT has six sections,

Observation – This section tests your ability to remember details

- **Alberta Police Communications Test (ACT)** – This section tests your ability to articulate in writing, complex thoughts in a clear and concise way that is understandable to others. This includes, vocabulary, spelling and English grammar.

- **Professional Judgment**

- **Recognition/Identification** – Here you are shown a face and asked to choose the same person from four pictures, where their appearance has been altered.

- **Logic** – This section tests your ability to analyze situations. Questions include, ordering pieces of information into a logical sequence, identifying patterns in data, and solving problems

- **Simple Word Problems** (Basic Math)

While we seek to make our guide as comprehensive as possible, note that like all exams, the APCAT Exam might be adjusted at some future point. New material might be added, or content that is no longer relevant or applicable might be removed. It is always a good idea to give the materials you receive when you register to take the APCAT test a careful review.

How this study guide is organized

This study guide is divided into three sections. The first section, Self-Assessments, will help you recognize your areas of strength and weakness. This will be a boon when it comes to managing your study time most efficiently; there is not much point of focusing on material you have already got firmly under control. Instead, taking the self-assessments will show you where that time could be much better spent. In this area you will begin with a few questions to evaluate quickly your understanding of material that is likely to appear on the APCAT test. If you do poorly in certain areas, simply work carefully through those sections in the tutorials and then try the self-assessment again.

The second section, Tutorials, offers information in each of the content areas, as well as strategies to help you master that material. The tutorials are not intended to be a complete course, but cover general principles. If you find that you do not understand the tutorials, it is recommended that you seek out additional instruction.

Third, we offer two sets of practice test questions, similar to those on the Alberta Police Exam.

The APCAT Study Plan

Now that you have made the decision to take the APCAT test, it is time to get started. Before you do another thing, you will need to figure out a plan of attack. The very best study tip is to start early! The longer the time period you devote to regular study practice, the more likely you will retain the material and access it quickly. If you thought that 1x20 is the same as 2x10, guess what? It really is not, when it comes to study time. Reviewing material for just an hour per day over the course of 20 days is far better than studying for two hours a day for only 10 days. The more often you revisit a particular piece of information, the better you will know it. Not only will your grasp and understanding be better, but your ability to reach into your brain and quickly and efficiently pull out the tidbit you need, will be greatly enhanced as well.

The great Chinese scholar and philosopher Confucius believed that true knowledge could be defined as knowing what you know and what you do not know. The first step in preparing for the APCAT is to assess your strengths and weaknesses. You may already have an idea of what you know and what you do not know, but evaluating yourself using our Self- Assessment modules for each of the test content areas may surprise you.

Making a Study Schedule
To make your study time the most productive, you will need to develop a study plan. The purpose of the plan is to organize all the bits of pieces of information in such a way that you will not feel overwhelmed. Rome was not built in a day, and learning everything you will need to know to pass the APCAT is going to take time, too. Arranging the material you need to learn into manageable chunks is the best way to go. Each study session should make you feel as though you have reached your goal, and your goal is simply to learn what you planned to learn during that particular session. Try to organize the content in such a way that each study session builds on previous ones. That way, you will retain the information, be better able to access it, and review the previous bits and pieces at the same time.

Self-assessment

The Best Study Tip! The very best study tip is to start early! The longer you study regularly, the more you will retain and 'learn' the material. Studying for 1 hour per day for 20 days is far better than studying for 2 hours for 10 days.

What don't you know?

The first step is to assess your strengths and weaknesses. You may already have an idea of where your weaknesses are, or you can take our Self-assessment modules for each of the content areas.

Exam Component	Rate 1 to 5
ACT	
Vocabulary	
Spelling	
English Grammar	
Professional Judgment	
Recognition/Identification	
Logic	
Identifying Patterns	
Solving Problems	
Basic Math	
Percent	
Decimals	
Word Problems	

Making a Study Schedule

The key to making a study plan is to divide the material you need to learn into manageable sized pieces and learn it, while at the same time reviewing the material that you already know.
Using the table above, any scores of 3 or below, you need to spend time learning, reviewing and practicing this subject area. A score of 4 means you need to review the material, but you don't have to re-learn it. A score of 5 and you are OK with just an occasional review before the exam.
A score of 0 or 1 means you really need to work on this should allocate the most time and the highest priority.
Some students prefer a 5-day plan and others a 10-day plan. It also depends on how much time until the exam.

Here is an example of a 5-day plan based on an example from the table above:

Recognizing Patterns: 1- Study 1 hour everyday – review on last day
Vocabulary: 3 - Study 1 hour for 3 days then ½ hour a day, then review
Word Problems: 4 - Review every second day
Professional Judgment: 5 - Review for ½ hour every other day
Logic: 5 - Review for ½ hour every other day

Using this example, logic and professional judgment are good, and only need occasional review. Vocabulary is good and needs 'some' review. Recognizing Patterns is very weak and need most of your time. Based on this, here is a sample study plan:

Day	Subject	Time
Monday		
Study	Recognizing Patterns	1 hour
Study	Word Problems	1 hour
½ hour break		
Study	Vocabulary	1 hour
Review	Recognizing Patterns	½ hour
Tuesday		
Study	Recognizing Patterns	1 hour
Study	Word Problems	½ hour
½ hour break		
Study	Vocabulary	½ hour
Review	Professional Judgment	½ hour
Review	Logic	½ hour
Wednesday		
Study	Recognizing Patterns	1 hour
Study	Word Problems	½ hour
½ hour break		
Study	Vocabulary	½ hour
Review	Recognizing Patterns	½ hour
Thursday		
Study	Recognizing Patterns	½ hour
Study	Word Problems	½ hour
Review	Vocabulary	½ hour
½ hour break		
Review	Logic	½ hour
Review	Professional Judgment	½ hour
Friday		
Review	Recognizing Patterns	½ hour
Review	Word Problems	½ hour
Review	Vocabulary	½ hour
½ hour break		
Review	Professional Judgment	½ hour
Review	Logic	½ hour

Using this example, adapt the study plan to your own schedule. This schedule assumes 2 ½ - 3 hours available to study everyday for a 5 day period.

First, write out what you need to study and how much. Next figure out how many days before the test. Note, do NOT study on the last day before the test. On the last day before the test, you won't learn anything and will probably only confuse yourself.

Make a table with the days before the test and the number of hours you have available to study each day. We suggest working with 1 hour and ½ hour time slots.

Start filling in the blanks, with the subjects you need to study the most, getting the most time, and the most regular time slots (i.e. everyday) and the subjects that you know getting the least time (e.g. ½ hour every other day, or every 3rd day).

Tips for making a schedule

Once you make a schedule, stick with it! Make your study sessions reasonable. If you make a study schedule and don't stick with it, you set yourself up for failure. Instead, schedule study sessions that are a bit shorter and set yourself up for success! Make sure your study sessions are do-able. Studying is hard work, but after you pass, you can party and take a break!

Schedule breaks. Breaks are just as important as study time. Work out a rotation of studying and breaks that works for you.

Build up study time. If you find it hard to sit still and study for 1 hour straight through, build up to it. Start with 20 minutes, and then take a break. Once you get used to 20-minute study sessions, increase the time to 30 minutes. Gradually work you way up to 1 hour.

How to Make a Study Plan and Schedule
https://www.test-preparation.ca/make-study-plan/

40 minutes to 1 hour is optimal. Studying for longer than this is tiring and not productive. Studying for shorter isn't long enough to be productive.

Studying Math. Studying Math is different from studying other subjects because you use a different part of your brain. The best way to study math is to practice everyday. This will train your mind to think in a mathematical way. If you miss a day or days, the mathematical mind-set is gone, and you have to start all over again to build it up.

More on how to study math
https://www.test-preparation.ca/study-math/

How to Study
For more information, see our How to Study Guide at https://www.test-preparation.ca/learning-study/

Professional Judgment

This section contains an Professional Judgment self-assessment. The tutorials are designed to familiarize general principles and the self-assessment contains general questions similar to the questions likely to be on the exam, but are not intended to be identical to the exam questions.

The questions in the self-assessment are not the same as you will find on the exam - that would be too easy! And nobody knows what the questions will be and they change all the time. Mostly, the changes consist of substituting new questions for old, but the changes also can be new question formats or styles, changes to the number of questions in each section, changes to the time limits for each section, and combining sections. So the format and exact wording of the questions may differ slightly, and changes from year to year, if you can answer the questions below, you will have no problem with the Professional Judgment section.

Answer Sheet

	A	B	C	D
1	○	○	○	○
2	○	○	○	○
3	○	○	○	○
4	○	○	○	○
5	○	○	○	○
6	○	○	○	○

Scenario 1

Dispatch reports a complaint of noisy and unruly teenagers hanging on the street. You proceed immediately to the area alone. You park the car nearby and observe 10 or 12 teens on the sidewalk. They do not appear to be taking drugs or drinking.

1. What should you do first?

    a. Approach the group and arrest them right away.

    b. Call for backup.

    c. Return to the station as there are no crimes being committed.

    d. Approach and question the group alone.

Scenario 2

2. Dispatch replies that back up is on its way. You wait in the car until 2 officers arrive. What is your next course of action.

    a. Approach the group with the 2 backup officers and politely inform them there has been a noise complaint.

    b. With the back up officers, arrest all the teens.

    c. Approach the group alone with the two backup officers still in the car, and tell the group they will have to be more quiet.

    d. Divide the group into three and have each officer question one group.

3. The teenagers are a little hostile but are not committing any crime. What should you do?

    a. Arrest all of them.

    b. Repeat that there has been a noise complaint, and ask them to please be more quiet.

    c. Search the group for drugs.

    d. Leave the scene.

Scenario 3

You are called to a street lamp that has fallen across the street, partly blocking traffic. You are the first to arrive.

4. What is the first action that you should take?

    a. Report the fallen lamp to dispatch.

    b. Check the street lamp for exposed or loose wires that may be carrying current.

    c. Secure the area around the fallen street lamp with pylons to direct traffic around the lamp and give dispatch an update on the situation.

    d. Evacuate the neighborhood.

Scenario 4

5. You recognize a stolen car and confirm with dispatch you are following the car alone. The stolen car has 4 people in it and you are alone. What should you do?

    a. Pull the car over immediately

    b. Call for backup, giving your position and situation, and keep following the car

    c. Report the position and direction and stop following the car.

    d. Call for backup and keep following the car.

Scenario 5

6. You are called to a robbery and see two cars leaving the scene at high speed. You give chase, however, the cars are driving at very high speed and driving very dangerously.

What should you do?

    a. Call dispatch with as much information as possible

    b. Follow the cars and match their speed.

    c. Follow the cars at a high but safe speed, even if you fall behind

    c. Follow the cars but do not exceed the speed limit.

Answer Key

1. B

The safest course of action is to call for backup.

2. A

A low key and polite approach is best.

3. B

No crime is being committed, so there is no reason to arrest, and searching may antagonize them and the situation could deteriorate quickly if handled aggressively.

4. C

The first priority is to ensure safety and secure the area, then give dispatch an updated report. Inspecting the street light, beyond a quick inspection, is beyond your expertise and not your job. Better to wait for qualified people to arrive.

5. B

With four people in the car, pulling them over alone is not advised. The priority is to give dispatch the most information you can, and keep following the car.

6. C

One of your responsibilities is the safety, which includes yourself. In addition, a high speed chase could endanger innocent people. The best action is to follow the cars at a high but safe speed and update dispatch with a description of the cars and any other information you have.

How to Answer this type of Question

Answering professional judgment questions involves common sense and following a set of basic criteria.

1. Safety - Assisting victims of crime, and injured persons.

This is the first and most important duty. Assisting injured persons, includes other officers.

2. Following Instructions

In an emergency, others, who may see a larger picture that you cannot, are counting on you to follow their orders without question.

3. Protect Property - calming disorder

Protecting private and public property and calming disorder and one for key duties of a police officer.

4. Perform duties - Keep the Peace, enforce the law, maintain order.

Keeping the peace and enforcing the law are the primary duties of a police officer.

RECOGNITION AND IDENTIFICATION

THIS SECTION CONTAINS A SELF-ASSESSMENT AND A SHORT RECOGNITION AND IDENTIFICATION TUTORIAL. The tutorials are designed to familiarize general principles and the self-assessment contains general questions similar to the questions likely to be on the APCAT, but are not intended to be identical to the exam questions.

The questions below are not the same as you will find on the APCAT - that would be too easy! And nobody knows what the questions will be and they change all the time. Mostly the changes consist of substituting new questions for old, but the changes can be new question formats or styles, changes to the number of questions in each section, changes to the time limits for each section and combining sections. Below are general quantitative skills questions that cover the same areas as the APCAT. So the format and exact wording of the questions may differ slightly, and change from year to year, if you can answer the questions below, you will have no problem with this section of the APCAT entrance test.

RECOGNITION AND IDENTIFICATION   23

1. Choose the person that matches the suspect below.

a.    b.

c.    d.

2. Choose the person that matches the suspect below.

a.

b.

c.

d.

Answer Key

1. A

Choice A is the same person. Choice B looks like a good choice as they are both wearing hoodies - notice though, the cheek bones are much narrower. Choices C and D are different people - the shape of their heads is quite different.

2. D

Choice D is the same person with different hair and sunglasses. Choices A and C have narrower facial structure. Choice B has a wider facial structure.

How to Answer This Type of Question.

Like most (all) types of questions on the APCAT exam, practice practice practice! In recognizing and identifying a suspect, focus on what can't be changed - eye color, cheek bones, facial structure, identifying marks such as birthmarks. Tattoos and piercings are also a clue, though they leave a mark and can be covered up.

Here is an example:

Choose the person that matches the suspect below.

Facial Structure is noticeably thinner so it can't be the same person.

Facial structure is much wider so it can't be the same person.

Facial Structure is the same - clearly the same person wearing sunglasses.

Alberta Communications Test - ACT

This section contains an Alberta Communications Test Self-Assessment. The tutorials are designed to familiarize general principles and the self-assessment contains general questions similar to the questions likely to be on the exam, but are not intended to be identical to the exam questions. The tutorials are not designed to be a complete course, and it is assumed that students have some familiarity with English grammar and usage, spelling and vocabulary. If you do not understand parts of the tutorial, or find the tutorial difficult, it is recommended that you seek out additional instruction.

Tour of the ACT Content

Below is a detailed list of the topics likely to appear on the exam.

- Spelling

- Vocabulary

- English usage

- English grammar

The questions in the self-assessment are not the same as you will find on the exam - that would be too easy! And nobody knows what the questions will be and they change all the time. Mostly, the changes consist of substituting new questions for old, but the changes also can be new question formats or styles, changes to the number of questions in each section, changes to the time limits for each section, and combining sections. So the format and exact wording of the questions may differ slightly, and changes from year to year, if you can answer the questions below, you will have no problem with the ACT section.

ACT Self-Assessment

The purpose of the self-assessment is:

- Identify your strengths and weaknesses.
- Develop your personalized study plan (above)
- Get accustomed to the format
- Extra practice – the self-assessments are almost a full 3rd practice test!
- Provide a baseline score for preparing your study schedule.

Since this is a Self-assessment, and depending on how confident you are with ACT, timing yourself is optional. This self-assessment has 60 questions, so allow 30 minutes to complete.

Answer Sheet

	A	B	C	D	E		A	B	C	D	E
1	○	○	○	○	○	21	○	○	○	○	○
2	○	○	○	○	○	22	○	○	○	○	○
3	○	○	○	○	○	23	○	○	○	○	○
4	○	○	○	○	○	24	○	○	○	○	○
5	○	○	○	○	○	25	○	○	○	○	○
6	○	○	○	○	○	26	○	○	○	○	○
7	○	○	○	○	○	27	○	○	○	○	○
8	○	○	○	○	○	28	○	○	○	○	○
9	○	○	○	○	○	29	○	○	○	○	○
10	○	○	○	○	○	30	○	○	○	○	○
11	○	○	○	○	○						
12	○	○	○	○	○						
13	○	○	○	○	○						
14	○	○	○	○	○						
15	○	○	○	○	○						
16	○	○	○	○	○						
17	○	○	○	○	○						
18	○	○	○	○	○						
19	○	○	○	○	○						
20	○	○	○	○	○						

Fill in the Blanks

1. Our _____ to America by sea was not very comfortable.

    a. journey
    b. voyage
    c. travel
    d. none of the above

2. I do not want to _____ a friend like you.

    a. lose
    b. loose
    c. lost
    d. none of the above

3. This pain killer will _____ your pain.

    a. lesson
    b. lessen
    c. lesen
    d. leson

4. Collecting stamps, _____ and listening to shortwave radio were Rick's main hobbies.

    a. building models
    b. to build models
    c. having built models
    d. build models

Directions: Choose the correct version of the underlined word or phrase in the given sentence.

5. She is the <u>most cleverest</u> girl in the class.

    a. She is the most clever girl in the class.

    b. She is the cleverest girl in the class.

    c. She is the most cleverer girl in the class.

    d. None of the above.

6. He <u>lived</u> in California since 1995.

    a. He had lived in California since 1995.

    b. He has been living in California since 1995.

    c. He has living in California since 1995.

    d. None of the above.

7. Politics <u>are</u> his chief interest.

    a. Politics is his chief interest.

    b. Politics are his chief interests.

    c. Politics is his chief interests.

    d. The sentence is correct.

8. He is a <u>cowered</u> person.

    a. He is a cowardest person.

    b. He is a cowardly person.

    c. He is a coward person.

    d. The sentence is correct.

9. Choose the sentence with the correct grammar.

a. The man was asked to come with his daughter and her test results.

b. The man was asked to come with her daughter and her test results.

c. The man was asked to come with her daughter and our test results.

d. None of the above.

10. Choose the sentence with the correct grammar.

a. Neither of them came with their bicycle.

b. Neither of them came with his bicycle.

c. Neither of them came with our bicycle.

d. None of the above.

11. Choose the correct spelling.

a. Weather

b. Weathur

c. Wether

d. None of the above

12. Choose the correct spelling.

a. Withdrawl

b. Withdrawal

c. Withdrawel

d. Witdrawal

13. Choose the correct spelling.

    a. Yatch
    b. Yache
    c. Yaute
    d. Yacht

14. Choose the correct spelling.

    a. Yeild
    b. Yielde
    c. Yield
    d. Yeelde

15. Choose the correct spelling.

    a. Warrant
    b. Warrent
    c. Warent
    d. Warant

16. Choose the correct spelling.

    a. Thorou
    b. Thurough
    c. Thorough
    d. Thorogh

17. Choose the correct spelling.

    a. Tomorow
    b. Tomorrow
    c. Tommorow
    d. Tommorrow

18. Choose the correct spelling.

   a. Unicke
   b. Uniqe
   c. Unique
   d. None of the Above

19. Choose the correct spelling.

   a. Unice
   b. Usable
   c. Ussable
   d. Usabble

20. Choose the correct spelling.

   a. Usually
   b. Usualy
   c. Ususally
   d. Ussually

Fill in the Blank.

21. When Joe broke his _____ in a skiing accident, his entire leg was in a cast.

   a. Ankle
   b. Humerus
   c. Wrist
   d. Femur

22. Alan had to learn the _____ system of numbering when his family moved to Great Britain.

    a. American

    b. Decimal

    c. Metric

    d. Fingers and toes

23. After Lisa's aunt had her tenth child, Lisa found that she had more than twenty _____.

    a. Uncles

    b. Friends

    c. Stepsisters

    d. Cousins

24. She was a rabid Red Sox fan, attending every game, and demonstrating her _____ by cheering more loudly than anyone else.

    a. Knowledge

    b. Boredom

    c. Commitment

    d. Enthusiasm

25. When Craig's dog was struck by a car, he rushed his pet to the _____.

    a. Emergency room

    b. Doctor

    c. Veterinarian

    d. Podiatrist

26. Gasoline is very _____.

   a. Volatile
   b. Flammable
   c. Inert
   d. None of the above

27. The tree has _____ over millions of years.

   a. Scared
   b. Petrified
   c. Rotted
   d. None of the above

28. They always get along and never _____.

   a. Bicker
   b. Socialize
   c. Debate
   d. None of the above

29. Her reputation as a _____ often gets her into trouble.

   a. Maverick
   b. Conformist
   c. Insider
   d. None of the above

30. Don't worry it will _____ in a few minutes.

   a. Degenerate
   b. Dissipate
   c. Scatter
   d. None of the above

Answer Key

1. B
"Travel" is a verb meaning to go from one place to another. A "journey" is a noun that refers to the travel event. A "voyage" is a journey by sea.

2. A
"Lose" is a verb meaning to misplace something or to fail at a competition. "Loose" is an adjective meaning untied or able to move freely.

3. B
"Lessen" means to reduce in size or intensity. "Lesson" refers to a formal time period in which particular information is taught or learned.

4. A
Present progressive "building models" is correct in this sentence.

5. B
Cleverest is the proper form to express 'most clever.'

6. B
Past perfect continuous, has been living, is proper because the time element, since 1995, and he is still living there now.

7. A
In spite of the 's' ending, "politics" is a singular noun.

8. B
"Cowardly" is an adjective used to modify a person.

9. A
A Pronoun should conform to its antecedent in gender, number and person.

10. B
Words such as neither, each, many, either, every, everyone, everybody and any should take a singular pronoun. Here

we are assuming the subject is male, and so use "his." The subject could be female, in which case we would use "her," however that is not one of the choices here.

11. A
Weather is the correct spelling.

12. B
Withdrawal is the correct spelling.

13. D
Yacht is the correct spelling.

14. C
Yield is the correct spelling.

15. A
Warrant is the correct spelling.

16. C
Thorough is the correct spelling.

17. B
Tomorrow is the correct spelling.

18. C
Unique is the correct spelling.

19. B
Usable is the correct spelling.

20. A
Usually is the correct spelling.

21. D
Femur NOUN the bone of the thigh or upper hind limb, articulating at the hip and the knee.

22. C
Metric System NOUN the decimal measuring system based on the meter, litre, and gram as units of length, capacity, and weight or mass.

23. D
Cousin NOUN a child of one's uncle or aunt.

24. D
Enthusiasm NOUN intense and eager enjoyment, interest, or approval.

25. C
Veterinarian NOUN a person qualified to treat diseased or injured animals.

26. A
Volatile Adjective ordinary, dull; everyday; unexceptional. (2) a person walking along a road or in a developed area.

27. B
Petrified ADJECTIVE changed to stone

28. A
Bicker VERB to quarrel in a tiresome, insulting manner.

29. A
Maverick NOUN showing independence in thoughts or actions.

30. B
Dissipate VERB to disperse or scatter.

English Grammar and Punctuation Tutorials

Capitalization

Although many of the rules for capitalization are pretty straight forward, there are several tricky points that are important to review.

Starting a Sentence

Everyone knows that you need to capitalize the first letter of the first word in a sentence, but is it really all that easy to figure out where one sentence starts and another stops? Take these three examples:

That was the moment it really sunk in: There would be no hockey this year.

It was April and that could mean only one thing: baseball.

We played for hours before heading home; everyone felt tired and happy.

In the first example, the first letter after the colon is capitalized, while in the second example it is not. That is because everything after the first example's colon is a complete sentence, while after example two's colon there is only one word. In example three you have what could be a complete sentence ("everyone felt tired and happy"), but which is not because it follows a semicolon, making it just another clause instead.

Within a sentence you can have an additional complete sentence if the sentence follows a colon. However, if what could be a complete sentence follows a semicolon, it is a clause, and is not capitalized.

Remember that the same rules apply for quotation marks that apply for colons: A complete sentence inside quotation marks is capitalized, but a single word or phrase is not.

Proper Nouns

The first letter of all proper nouns needs to be capitalized. There are many categories of proper noun. The most common proper nouns are specific names of people (such as Bill), places (such as Germany) or things (such as Honda Civic). However, there are several less obvious categories of words that should be capitalized as proper nouns.

Historical events such as World War II or the California Gold Rush need to be capitalized.

The names of celestial bodies such as Orion's Belt need to be capitalized.

The names of ethnicities such as African-American or Hispanic need to be capitalized.

Relationship words that replace a person's name such as Mom, Doctor and Mister need to be capitalized. However, this only happens when you use the word to replace the person's name. In the sentence, "My mom went to the store," you do not capitalize it, while in the sentence, "Hey Mom, did you get toothpaste at the store?" you do capitalize it.

Geographical locations are capitalized. This can get a little tricky because capitalized geographical locations and non-capitalized directions are easy to confuse. Saying, "We drove south for hours," is a direction, so the word "south" should not be capitalized. However, when saying, "While in the United States, we drove to the South to look at Civil War battle fields," you do capitalize the word "South." The difference is that in the first sentence "south" is just the direction you drove. In the second sentence "the South" is a specific region of the United States that formed itself into the Confederacy during the US Civil War.

Proper Adjectives

Proper adjectives are the adjective forms of proper nouns. People from Germany are German; people from Canada are Canadian. German and Canadian are proper adjectives because they are forms of proper nouns that are used to describe other nouns.

Titles of Works

Titles of works are generally capitalized following a specific pattern. Capitalize all of the important words in a sentence. Do not capitalize unimportant words such as prepositions and articles.

For example: Alien Spaceship Spotted over Many of the World's Capitals

Notice that the prepositions "over" and "of," and the article "the" are the only non-capitalized words in the sentence.

Colons and Semicolons

Within a sentence there are several different types of punctuation marks that can denote a pause. Each of these punctuation marks has different rules when it comes to its structure and usage, so we will look at each one in turn.

Colons

The colon is used primarily to introduce information. It can start lists such as in the sentence, "There were several things Susan had to get at the store: bread, cereal, lettuce and tomatoes." Or a colon points out specific information, such as in the sentence, "It was only then that the group fully realized what had happened: The Martian invasion had begun."

Note that if the information after the colon is a complete sentence, you capitalize and punctuate it exactly like you would a sentence. If, however, it does not constitute a complete sentence, you don't have to capitalize anything. ("Peering out the window Meredith saw them: zombies.")

Semicolons

Semicolons are super commas. They denote a stronger stop than a comma does, but they are still weaker than a period, not quite capable of ending a sentence. Semicolons are primarily used to separate independent clauses that are not being separated by a coordinating conjunction. ("Chris went to the store; he bought chips and salsa.") Semicolons can only do this, however, when the ideas in each clause are related. For instance, the sentence, "It's raining outside; my sister went to the movies," is not a proper usage of the semicolon since those clauses have nothing to do with each other.

Semicolons can also be used in lists if more element in the list is itself made up of a smaller list. If you want to write a list of things you plan to bring to a picnic, and those things only include a Frisbee, a chair and some pasta salad, you would not need to use a semicolon. But if you also wanted to bring plastic knives, forks and spoons, you would need to write your sentence like this: "For our picnic I am bringing a Frisbee; a chair; plastic knives, forks and spoons; and some pasta salad."

Using semicolons like this preserves the smaller list that you have in your larger list.

Commas

Commas are probably the most commonly used punctuation mark in English. Commas can break the flow of writing to give it a more natural sounding style, and they are the main punctuation mark used to separate ideas. Commas also separate lists, introductory adverbs, introductory prepositional phrases, dates and addresses.

The most rigid way that commas are used is when separating clauses. There are two primary types of clauses in a sentence, independent and subordinate (sometimes called dependent). Independent clauses are clauses that express a complete thought, such as, "Tim went to the store." Subordinate clauses, on the other hand, only express partial thoughts that expand on an independent clause, such as, "after the game ended," which you can see is clearly not a complete sentence. (You will learn more about clauses in different lessons.)

The rule for commas with clauses is that a comma must separate the clauses when a subordinate clause comes first in a sentence: "After the game ended, Tim went to the store." But there should not be a comma when a subordinate clause follows an independent clause: "Tim went to the store after the game ended." If you leave the comma out of the first example, you have a run-on sentence. If you add one into the second example, you have a comma-splice error. Also, when you have two independent clauses joined with a coordinating conjunction, you need to separate them with a comma. "Tim went to the store, and Beth went home."

There are some artistic exceptions to these rules, such as adding a pause for literary effect, but for the most part, they are set in stone.

Commas are also used to separate items in a list. This area of English is unfortunately less clear than it should be, with two separate rules depending on what standard you are following. To understand the two different rules, let's pretend you are having a party at your house, and you are making a list of refreshments your friends will want. You may decide to serve three things: 1) pizza 2) chips 3) drinks. There are two different rules governing how you should punctuate this. According to many grammar books, you would write this as, "At the store I will buy pizza, chips, and drinks."

This variation puts a comma after each item in the list. It is the version that the style books used in most college English and history courses will prefer, so it is probably the one you should follow. However, the Associated Press style guide, which is used in college journalism classes and at newspapers and magazines, says the sentence should be written like this: "At the store I will buy pizza, chips and drinks." Here you only use a comma between the first two words, letting the word "and" act as the separator between the last two.

Another important place to use commas is when you have a modifier that describes an element of a sentence, but that does not directly follow the thing it describes. Look at the sentence: "Tim went over to visit Beth, watching the full moon along the way." In this sentence there is no confusion about who is "watching the full moon"; it is Tim, probably as he walks to Beth's house. If you remove the comma, however, you get this: "Tim went over to visit Beth watching the full moon along the way." Now it sounds as though Beth is watching the full moon, and we are forced to wonder what "way" the moon is traveling along.

Commas are also used when adding introductory prepositional phrases and introductory adverbs to sentences. A comma is always needed following an introductory adverb. ("Quickly, Jody ran to the car.") Commas are even necessary when you have an adverb introducing a clause within a sentence, even if the clause not the first clause of the sentence. ("Amanda wanted to go to the movie; however, she knew her homework was more important.")

With introductory prepositional phrases you only add a comma if the phrase (or if a group of introductory phrases) is five or more words long. Thus, the sentence you just read did not have a comma following its introductory prepositional phrase ("With introductory prepositional phrases") because it was only four words. Compare that to this sentence with a five word introductory phrase: "After the ridiculously long class, the friends needed to relax."

The last way commas are used in sentences is to separate information that does not need to be there. For instance, "My cousin Hector, who wore a blue hat at the party, thought you were funny." The fact that Hector wore a blue hat is interesting, but it is not vital to the sentence; it could be removed and not changed the sentence's meaning. Therefore, it gets commas around it. Along these lines you should remember that any clause introduced by the word that is considered to provide essential information to the sentence and should not get commas around it. Conversely, any clause starting with the word which is considered nonessential and should not get commas around it.

Quotation Marks

Quotation marks are used in English in a variety of different ways. The most common use of quotation marks is to show quotations either, as dialogue or, when directly quoting a source in an essay or news article. Fortunately, both of these uses follow the same basic rules.

When you have a quote written as the second part of a sentence, you need to put a comma before the quotation marks and a period inside the quotation marks at the end. (Franklin said, "Let's go to the store.") Conversely, when you have quote as the first part of the sentence with information describing it second, a comma replaces the period at the end of the sentence inside the quotes. ("Let's go to the store," Franklin said.)

If the information in a quote is not a complete sentence, you do not need to capitalize it or put commas around it, if it is not dialogue. (No one thought the idea of "going to the store" sounded very fun.)

Note that when the last word in a sentence has both a quotation mark and a period attached to it, the period is always inside the quotes. This is the case when you have a complete sentence inside a quote ("Let's go to the store."), and when the last word in a sentence just happens to have quote marks around it (Kerri said I was "mean.") You also need to do the same thing with commas. (Kerri said I was "mean," and it made me feel bad.) However, other punctuation marks such as colons, semicolons and dashes do not follow this rule and should come outside the quotes. (Kerri said I was "mean"; it made me feel bad.)

When you want to use a quote inside a quote, you use the standard double-quotation marks for the outer quote and single-quotation marks for the inner quote. ("The sign on the door said 'no soliciting,' so we went to the next house.")

Quotation marks are also used around certain types of titles. To figure out which ones, it helps to look at which titles are not put in quotes as well.

Titles are generally in two categories: large works and small works. Large works are things such as newspapers, magazines, CDs, books and television shows. The defining characteristic of a large work is that it is able to hold small works in it. Small works are the articles inside newspapers and magazines, the songs on a CD, the chapters in a book and the episodes of a television show. It is small works that get quotation marks around them. (Large works, meanwhile, are either underlined or italicized.)

Using quotation marks correctly in a title looks something like this: The two-page article entitled "San Francisco Giants Win World Series" appeared in yesterday's New York Times. The article title is in quotes, and the newspaper title is in italics.

Common English Usage Mistakes - A Quick Review

Like some parts of English grammar, usage is definitely going to be on the exam and there isn't any tricky strategies or shortcuts to help you get through this section.

Here is a quick review of common usage mistakes.

1. May and Might

'May' can act as a principal verb, which can express permission or possibility.

Examples:

Lets wait, the meeting may have started.
May I begin now?

'May' can act as an auxiliary verb, which an expresses a purpose or wish

Examples:

May you find favour in the sight of your employer.
May your wishes come true.
People go to school so that they may be educated.

The past tense of may is might.

Examples:

I asked if I might begin

'Might' can be used to signify a weak or slim possibility or polite suggestion.

Examples:

You might find him in his office, but I doubt it.
You might offer to help if you want to.

2. Lie and Lay

The verb lay should always take an object. The three forms of the verb lay are: laid, lay and laid.

The verb lie (recline) should not take any object. The three forms of the verb lie are: lay, lie and lain.

Examples:

Lay on the bed.
The tables were laid by the students.
Let the little kid lie.
The patient lay on the table.

The dog has lain there for 30 minutes.

Note: The verb lie can also mean "to tell a falsehood." This verb can appear in three forms: lied, lie, and lied. This is different from the verb lie (recline) mentioned above.

Examples:

The accused is fond of telling lies.
Did she lie?

3. Would and should

The past tense of shall is 'should', and so "should" generally follows the same principles as "shall."

The past tense of will is "would," and so "would" generally follows the same principles as "will."

The two verbs 'would and should' can be correctly used interchangeably to signify obligation. The two verbs also have some unique uses too. Should is used in three persons to signify obligation.

Examples:

I should go after work.
People should do exercises everyday.
You should be generous.

"Would" is specially used in any of the three persons, to signify willingness, determination and habitual action.

Examples:

They would go for a test run every Saturday.
They would not ignore their duties.
She would try to be punctual.

4. Principle and Auxiliary Verbs

Two principal verbs can be used along with one auxiliary verb when the auxiliary verb form suits the two principal verbs.

Examples:

A number of people have been employed and some promoted.

A new tree has been planted and the old has been cut down.
Again note the difference in the verb form.

5. Can and Could

A. Can is used to express capacity or ability.

Examples:

I can complete the assignment today
He can meet up with his target.

B. Can is also used to express permission.

Examples:

Yes, you can begin

In the sentence below, "can" was used to mean the same thing as "may." However, the difference is that the word "can" is used for negative or interrogative sentences, while "may" is used in affirmative sentences to express possibility.

Examples:

They may be correct.   Positive sentence - use may.
Can this statement be correct? A question using "can."
It cannot be correct. Negative sentence using "can."

The past tense of can is could. It can serve as a principal verb when it is used to express its own meaning.

Examples:

Despite the difficulty of the test, he could still perform well. "Could" here is used to express ability.

6. Ought

The verb ought should normally be followed by the word to.

Examples:

I *ought to* close shop now.

The verb 'ought' can be used to express:

A. Desirability

You ought to wash your hands before eating. It is desirable to wash your hands.

B. Probability

She ought to be on her way back by now. She is probably on her way.

C. Moral obligation or duty

The government ought to protect the oppressed. It is the government's duty to protect the oppressed.

7. Raise and Rise

Rise

The verb rise means to go up, or to ascend.
The verb rise can appear in three forms, rose, rise, and risen. The verb should not take an object.

Examples:

The bird rose very slowly.
The trees rise above the house.

My aunt has risen in her career.

Raise

The verb raise means to increase, to lift up.
The verb raise can appear in three forms, raised, raise and raised.

Examples:

He raised his hand.
The workers requested a raise.

Do not raise that subject.

8. Past Tense and Past Participle

Pay attention to the proper use these verbs: sing, show, ring, awake, fly, flow, begin, hang and sink.
Mistakes usually occur when using the past participle and past tense of these verbs as they are often mixed up.

Each of these verbs can appear in three forms:

Sing, Sang, Sung.
Show, Showed, Showed/Shown.
Ring, Rang, Rung.
Awake, awoke, awaken
Fly, Flew, Flown.
Flow, Flowed, Flowed.
Begin, Began, Begun.
Hang, Hanged, Hanged (a criminal)
Hang, Hung, Hung (a picture)
Sink, Sank, Sunk.

Examples:

The stranger rang the door bell. (simple past tense)
I have rung the door bell already. (past participle - an action completed in the past)

The stone sank in the river. (simple past tense)
The stone had already sunk. (past participle - an action completed in the past)

The meeting began at 4:00.
The meeting has begun.

9. Shall and Will

When speaking informally, the two can be used interchangeably. In formal writing, they must be used correctly.

"Will" is used in the second or third person, while "shall" is used in the first person. Both verbs are used to express a time or even in the future.

Examples:

I shall, We shall (First Person)
You will (Second Person)
They will (Third Person)

This principle however reverses when the verbs are to be used to express threats, determination, command, willingness, promise or compulsion. In these instances, will is now used in first person and shall in the second and third person.

Examples:

I will be there next week, no matter what.
This is a promise, so the first person "I" takes "will."

You shall ensure that the work is completed.
This is a command, so the second person "you" takes "shall."

I will try to make payments as promised.
This is a promise, so the first person "I" takes "will."

They shall have arrived by the end of the day.
This is a determination, so the third person "they" takes shall.

Note

A. The two verbs, shall and will, should not occur twice in the same sentence when the same future is being referred to

Example:

I shall arrive early if my driver is here on time.

B. Will should not be used in the first person when questions are being asked

Examples:

Shall I go?
Shall we go?

SUBJECT VERB AGREEMENT

Verbs in any sentence must agree with the subject of the sentence both in person and number. Problems usually occur when the verb doesn't correspond with the right subject or the verb fails to match the noun close to it.

Unfortunately, there is no easy way around these principals - no tricky strategy or easy rule. You just have to memorize them.

Here is a quick review:

The verb to be, present (past)

Person	Singular	Plural
First	I am (was)	we are (were)
Second	you are (were)	you are (were)
Third	he, she, it is (was)	they are (were)

The verb to have, present (past)

Person	Singular	Plural
First	I have (had)	we have (had)
Second	you have (had)	you have (had)
Third	he, she, it has (had)	they have (had)

Regular verbs, e.g. to walk, present (past)

Person	Singular	Plural
First	I walk (walked)	we walk (walked)
Second	you walk (walked)	you walk (walked)
Third	he, she, it walks (walked)	they work (walked)

1. Every and Each

When nouns are qualified by "every" or "each," they take a singular verb even if they are joined by 'and'

Examples:

Each mother and daughter was a given separate test.
Every teacher and student was properly welcomed.

2. Plural Nouns

Nouns like measles, tongs, trousers, riches, scissors etc. are all plural.
Examples:

The trousers are dirty.
My scissors have gone missing.
The tongs are on the table.

3. With and As Well

Two subjects linked by "with" or "as well" should have a verb that matches the first subject.

Examples:

The pencil, with the papers and equipment, is on the desk.
David as well as Louis is coming.

4. Plural Nouns

The following nouns take a singular verb:

politics, mathematics, innings, news, advice, summons, furniture, information, poetry, machinery, vacation, scenery

Examples:

The machinery is difficult to assemble
The furniture has been delivered
The scenery was beautiful

5. Single Entities

A proper noun in plural form that refers to a single entity requires a singular verb. This is a complicated way of saying; some things appear to be plural, but are really singular, or some nouns refer to a collection of things but the collection is really singular.

Examples:

The United Nations Organization is the decision maker in the matter.

Here the "United Nations Organization" is really only one "thing" or noun, but is made up of many "nations."

The book, "The Seven Virgins" was not available in the library.
Here there is only one book, although the title of the book is plural.

6. Specific Amounts are always singular

A plural noun that refers to a specific amount or quantity that is considered as a whole (dozen, hundred, score etc) requires a singular verb.

Examples:

60 minutes is quite a long time.
Here "60 minutes" is considered a whole, and therefore one item (singular noun).

The first million is the most difficult.

7. Either, Neither and Each are always singular

The verb is always singular when used with: either, each, neither, everyone and many.

Examples:

Either of the boys is lying.
Each of the employees has been well compensated
Many a police officer has been found to be courageous
Every one of the teachers is responsible

8. Linking with Either, Or, and Neither match the second subject

Two subjects linked by "either," "or,""nor" or "neither" should have a verb that matches the second subject.

Examples:

Neither David nor Paul will be coming.
Either Mary or Tina is paying.
Note
If one subject linked by "either," "or,""nor" or "neither" is in plural form, then the verb should also be in plural, and the verb should be close to the plural subject.

Examples:
Neither the mother nor her kids have eaten.
Either Mary or her friends are paying.

9. Collective Nouns are Plural

Some collective nouns such as poultry, gentry, cattle, vermin etc. are considered plural and require a plural verb.

Examples:

The poultry are sick.
The cattle are well fed.

Note
Collective nouns involving people can work with both plural and singular verbs.
Examples:

Nigerians are known to be hard working
Europeans live in Africa

10. Nouns that are Singular and Plural

Nouns like deer, sheep, swine, salmon etc. can be singular or plural and require the same verb form.

Examples:

The swine is feeding. (singular)
The swine are feeding. (plural)

The salmon is on the table. (singular)
The salmon are running upstream. (plural)

11. Collective Nouns are Singular

Collective nouns such as Army, Jury, Assembly, Committee, Team etc should carry a singular verb when they subscribe to one idea. If the ideas or views are more than one, then the verb should be plural.

Examples:

The committee is in agreement in their decision.

The committee were in disagreement in their decision.
The jury has agreed on a verdict.
The jury were unable to agree on a verdict.

12. Subjects links by "and" are plural.

Two subjects linked by "and" always require a plural verb

Examples:

David and John are students.

Note
If the subjects linked by "and" are used as one phrase, or constitute one idea, then the verb must be singular

The color of his socks and shoe is black.
Here "socks and shoe" are two nouns, however the subject is "color" which is singular.

MATHEMATICS

This section contains a self-assessment and math tutorials. The tutorials are designed to familiarize general principles and the self-assessment contains general questions similar to the math questions likely to be on the exam, but are not intended to be identical to the exam questions. The tutorials are not designed to be a complete math course, and it is assumed that students have some familiarity with math. If you do not understand parts of the tutorial, or find the tutorial difficult, it is recommended that you seek out additional instruction.

Tour of the APCAT Mathematics Content

Below is a detailed list of the mathematics topics likely to appear on the exam. Make sure that you understand these topics at the very minimum.

- Convert decimals, percent, roman numerals and fractions

- Solve word problems

- Calculate percent and ratio

- Operations using fractions, percent and fractions

- Analyze and interpret tables, graphs and charts

- Understand and solve simple algebra problems

- Simple Geometry

The questions in the self-assessment are not the same as you will find on the exam - that would be too easy! And nobody knows what the questions will be and they change all the time. Mostly, the changes consist of substituting new questions for old, but the changes also can be new question formats or styles, changes to the number of questions in each section, changes to the time limits for each section, and combining sections. So, while the format and exact wording of the questions may differ slightly, and changes from year to year, if you can answer the questions below, you will have no problem with the mathematics section.

Mathematics Self-Assessment

The purpose of the self-assessment is:

- Identify your strengths and weaknesses.
- Develop your personalized study plan (above)
- Get accustomed to the format
- Extra practice – the self-assessments are almost a full 3rd practice test!
- Provide a baseline score for preparing your study schedule.

Since this is a Self-assessment, and depending on how confident you are with Math, timing yourself is optional. This self-assessment has 15 questions, so allow about 15 minutes to complete.

Once complete, use the table below to assess your understanding of the content, and prepare your study schedule described in chapter 1.

80% - 100%	Excellent – you have mastered the content
60 – 79%	Good. You have a working knowledge. Even though you can just pass this section, you may want to review the tutorials and do some extra practice to see if you can improve your mark.
40% - 59%	Below Average. You do not understand the content. Review the tutorials, and retake this quiz again in a few days, before proceeding to the Practice Test Questions.
Less than 40%	Poor. You have a very limited understanding. Please review the tutorials, and retake this quiz again in a few days, before proceeding to the Practice Test Questions.

Math Self-Assessment Answer Sheet

	A	B	C	D
1	○	○	○	○
2	○	○	○	○
3	○	○	○	○
4	○	○	○	○
5	○	○	○	○
6	○	○	○	○
7	○	○	○	○
8	○	○	○	○
9	○	○	○	○
10	○	○	○	○
11	○	○	○	○
12	○	○	○	○
13	○	○	○	○

Math Self-Assessment

1. A motorcycle is traveling at 100 km/hr. How far will it travel in 2 minutes?

    a. 1.6
    b. 3.3
    c. 1
    d. 12.5

2. Bill invests $4,000 at 8% compounded yearly. How much will he have in 2 years?

    a. $4320.00
    b. $4665.60
    c. $4640.00
    d. $4800.00

3. A waitress serves 10 tables one evening on her shift from 6 - 12:00 PM. She makes $10.50 per hour plus tips. Her total bills come to $240.60 with an average tip of 12%. How much did she make?

    a. $28.87
    b. $63.00
    c. $91.87
    d. $81.87

4. 15 is what percent of 200?

    a. 7.5%
    b. 15%
    c. 20%
    d. 17.50%

5. A boy has 5 red balls, 3 white balls and 2 yellow balls. What percent of the balls are yellow?

  a. 2%
  b. 8%
  c. 20%
  d. 12%

6. Add 10% of 300 to 50% of 20

  a. 50%
  b. 40%
  c. 60%
  d. 45%

7. Convert 75% to a fraction.

  a. 2/100
  b. 75/100
  c. 3/4
  d. 4/7

8. Convert 90% to a fraction

  a. 1/10
  b. 9/9
  c. 10/100
  d. 9/10

9. A man buys an item for $420 and has a balance of $3000.00. How much did he have before?

  a. $2,580
  b. $3,420
  c. $2,420
  d. $342

10. Divide 9.60 by 3.2

    a. 2.50
    b. 3
    c. 2.3
    d. 6.4

11. If X = 7 solve 3x + 5 – 2x

    a. x = 6
    b. x = 12
    c. x = 1
    d. x = 0

12. Solve $\sqrt{121}$

    a. 11
    b. 23
    c. 12
    d. 9

13. Solve 3x – 27 = 0

    a. x = 24
    b. x = 30
    c. x = 9
    d. x = 21

Answer Key

1. B
First calculate the distance traveled in 1 minute.
100 km/hr. = 100/60 = 1.666 km/minute.
So, in 2 minutes the motorcycle will travel 3.33 kilometers.

2. B
For the first year, $4,000 invested at 8% will be 4000 X .08 = 320. The interest is compounded yearly, so to calculate the second years interest, 4320 X .08 = 345.60.
The total will then be 4320 + 345.60 = $4665.60

3. C
First calculate her hourly wage. 6 hours X 10.50/hour = $63. Next calculate tips. $240.60 X .12 = $28.87. So her total earnings will be 63 + 28.87 = 91.87

4. A
15% = 15/100 X 200 = 7.5%

5. C
Total no. of balls = 10, no. of yellow balls = 2. 2/10 X 100 = 20%

6. B
10% of 300 = 30 and 50% of 20 = 10 so 30 + 10 = 40.

7. C
75% = 75/100 = 3/4

8. D
90% = 90/100 = 9/10

9. B
(Amount Spent) $420 + $3000 (Balance) = $3,420

10. B
9.60/3.2 = 3

11. B
X = 7, so 3x = 3 x 7 = 21, 2x = 2 x 7 = 14, so 21 + 5 - 14 = 26 - 14 = 12

12. A
$\sqrt{121} = 11$

13. C
3x = 27, x = 27/3, x = 9

Basic Math Video Tutorials

https://www.test-preparation.ca/math-videos/

Fraction Tips, Tricks and Shortcuts

When you are writing an exam, time is precious, so anything you can do to answer questions faster is a real advantage.

Here are some ideas, shortcuts, tips and tricks that can speed up answering fraction problems.

Remember that a fraction is just a number which names a portion of something. For instance, instead of having a whole pie, a fraction says you have a part of a pie--such as a half of one or a fourth of one.

Two numbers make up a fraction. The number on top is the numerator. The number on the bottom is the denominator.

To remember which is which, just remember that "denominator" and "down" both start with a "d." And the "downstairs" number is the denominator. So for instance, in ½, the numerator is 1, and the denominator (or "downstairs") number is 2.

Adding Fractions

It's easy to add two fractions if they have the same denominator. Just add the digits on top and leave the bottom one the same: 1/10 + 6/10 = 7/10.

It's the same with subtracting fractions with the same denominator: 7/10 - 6/10 = 1/10.

Adding and subtracting fractions with different denominators is more complicated.

First, you have to arrange the fractions so they have the same denominators.

The easiest way to do this is to multiply the denominators: For 2/5 + 1/2 multiply 5 by 2. Now you have a denominator of 10.

But now you have to change the top numbers too. Since you multiplied the 5 in 2/5 by 2, you also multiply the 2 by 2, to get 4. So the first fraction is now 4/10.

In the second fraction, you multiplied the denominator by 5, you have to multiply the numerator by 5 also, to get 5/10.

Now you have 4/10 + 5/10 and you can add 5 and 4 to get 9/10.

Simplest Form

To reduce a fraction to its simplest form, you have to arrange the numerator and denominator so the only common factor is 1.

Think of it this way:

Let's take an example: The fraction 2/10.

This is not reduced to its simplest terms because there is a number that will divide evenly into both: 2. We want to make it so that the only number that will divide evenly into both is 1.

Divide the top and bottom by 2 to get the new, reduced fraction - 1/5.

Multiplying Fractions

This is the easiest of all: Just multiply the two top numbers and then multiply the two bottom numbers.

Here is an example,

2/5 X 2/3

First, multiply the numerators: 2 X 2 = 4

then multiply the denominators: 5 X 3 = 15

Your answer is 4/15.

Dividing Fractions

Dividing fractions is easy if you remember a simple trick - first turn the second fraction upside down - then multiply!

Here is an example:

7/8 X 1/2

Turn the second fraction upside down:

7/8 X 2/1

then multiply:

(7 X 2) / (8 X 1) = 14/8

Converting Fractions to Decimals

There are a couple of ways to convert fractions to decimals. The first, which is the fastest -- is to memorize some basic fraction facts.

1/100 is "one hundredth," expressed as a decimal, it's .01.

> 1/50 is "two hundredths," expressed as a decimal, it's .02.
>
> 1/25 is "one twenty-fifth" or "four hundredths," expressed as a decimal, it's .04.
>
> 1/20 is "one twentieth" or ""five hundredths," ex-

pressed as a decimal, it's .05.

1/10 is "one tenth," expressed as a decimal, it's .1.

1/8 is "one eighth," or "one hundred twenty-five thousandths," expressed as a decimal, it's .125.

1/5 is "one fifth," or "two tenths," expressed as a decimal, it's .2.

1/4 is "one fourth" or "twenty-five hundredths," expressed as a decimal, it's .25.

1/3 is "one third" or "thirty-three hundredths," expressed as a decimal, it's .33.

1/2 is "one half" or "five tenths," expressed as a decimal, it's .5.

3/4 is "three fourths," or "seventy-five hundredths," expressed as a decimal, it's .75.

Of course, if you're no good at memorization, another good technique for converting a fraction to a decimal is to manipulate it so that the fraction's denominator is 10, 100, 1000, or some other power of 10.

Here's an example: We'll start with three quarters. What is the first number in the 4 "times table" that you can multiply and get a multiple of 10? Can you multiply 4 by something to get 10? No. Can you multiply it by something to get 100? Yes! 4 X 25 is 100.

So multiply the numerator by 25, which is 75 over 100

We know fractions are really a division problem, and we also know that dividing by 100, means we move the decimal 2 places to the left.

So, 75 over 100 = .75

Lets try another example - Convert one fifth to a decimal.

First find a power of 10 that 5 goes into evenly, which is 2.

Multiply the numerator and denominator by 2, which is two tenths.

Dividing 2 by 10 means we move the decimal place 1 place to the left.

So one fifth = zero point two

Converting Fractions to Percent

Here is a quick method to convert fraction to percent and a strategy for answering on a multiple choice test that will save you valuable exam time.

First, remember that a fraction is a division problem: you're dividing the bottom number into the top.

Taking an example, convert 2/3 into percent.

The first method is to multiple the numerator by 100 and divide. So,
(2 X 100) / 2 = 100/3 = 66.66

Add a % sign and you have the answer, 66.66%

If you're doing these conversions on a multiple-choice test, here's an idea that might be even easier and faster. Let's say you have a fraction of 1/8 and you're asked to convert to percent.

Since we know that "percent" means hundredths, ask yourself what number we can multiply 8 by to get 100. Since there is no number, ask what number gets us close to 100.

That number is 12: 8 X 12 = 96. So it gets us a little less than 100. Now, whatever you do to the denominator, you have to do to the numerator. Let's multiply 1 X 12 and we get 12. However, since 96 is a little less than 100, we know that our answer will be a little MORE than 12%.

Look at the choices and eliminate the obvious wrong choices. So if your possible answers on the multiple-choice test are these:

a) 8.5% b) 19% c) 12.5% d) 25%

then we know the answer is c) 12.5%, because it's a little MORE than the 12 we got in our math problem above.

Here all the choices except choice C 12.5% can be eliminated.

You don't have to know the exact correct answer, just enough to estimate, then eliminate the obviously wrong answers.

This was an easy example to demonstrate the strategy, but don't be fooled! You probably won't get such an easy question on your exam. By estimating your answer quickly, then eliminating obviously incorrect choices immediately, you save precious exam time.

DECIMAL TIPS, TRICKS AND SHORT-CUTS

Converting Decimals to Fractions

Converting decimals to fractions is easy if you say it the right way! If you say "point one" or "point 25," you'll have trouble.

But if you say, "one tenth" and "twenty-five hundredths," then you have already solved it! That's because, if you know your fractions, you know that "one tenth" looks like this: 1/10. And "twenty-five hundredths" looks like this: 25/100.

Even if you have digits before the decimal, such as 3.4, learning how to say the word will help you with the conversion into a fraction. It's not "three point four," it's "three and four tenths." Knowing this, you know that the fraction which looks like "three and four tenths" is 3 4/10.

The conversion is not complete until you reduce the fraction to its lowest terms: It's not 25/100, but 1/4.

Converting Decimals to Percent

Changing a decimal to a percent is easy if you remember one thing: multiply by 100.

For example, if you start with .45, simply multiply it by 100 for 45. Then add the % sign to the end - 45%.

Think of it this way: take out the decimal point, add a percent sign on the opposite side. In other words, the decimal on the left is replaced by the % on the right.

It doesn't work quite that easily if the decimal is in the middle of the number. For example, 3.7. Here, take out the decimal in the middle and replace it with a 0 % at the end.

So 3.7 converted to decimal is 370%.

Percent Tips, Tricks and Shortcuts

Percent problems are not nearly as scary as they appear, if you remember this neat trick:

Draw a cross as in:

Portion	Percent
Whole	100

In the upper left, write PORTION. In the bottom left, write WHOLE. In the top right, write PERCENT and in the bottom right, write 100. Whatever your problem is, you will leave blank the unknown, and fill in the other four parts. For example, let's suppose your problem is: Find 10% of 50. Since we know the 10% part, we put 10 in the percent corner. Since the whole number in our problem is 50, we put that in the corner marked whole. You always put 100 underneath the percent, so we leave it as is, which leaves only the top left corner blank. This is where we'll put our answer. Now simply multiply the two corner numbers that are NOT 100. Here, it's 10 X 50. That gives us 500. Now divide this by the remaining corner, or 100, to get a final answer of 5. 5 is the number that goes in the upper-left corner, and is your final solution.

Another hint to remember: Percents are the same thing as hundredths in decimals. So .45 is the same as 45 hundredths or 45 percent.

Converting Percents to Decimals

Percents are just a type of decimal, so it should be no surprise that converting between the two is actually fairly simple. Here are a few tricks and shortcuts to keep in mind:

- ☐ Remember that percent literally means "per 100" or "for every 100." So when you speak of 30% you're saying 30 for every 100 or the fraction 30/100. In basic math, you learned that fractions that have 10 or 100 as the denominator can easily be turned to a decimal. 30/100 is thirty hundredths, or expressed as a decimal, .30.

- ☐ Another way to look at it: To convert a percent to a decimal, simply divide the number by 100. So for instance, if the percent is 47%, divide 47 by 100. The result will be .47. Get rid of the % mark and you're done.
- ☐ Remember that the easiest way of dividing by 100 is by moving your decimal two spots to the left.

Converting Percent to Fractions

Converting Percent to Fractions is easy. After all, a percent is just a type of fraction; it tells you what part of 100 that you're talking about. Here are some simple ideas for making the conversion from a percent to a fraction:

- ☐ If the percent is a whole number -- say 34% -- then simply write a fraction with 100 as the denominator (the bottom number). Then put the percentage itself on top. So 34% becomes 34/100.
- ☐ Now reduce as you would reduce any percent. Here, by dividing 2 into 34 and 2 into 100, you get 17/50.
- ☐ If your percent is not a whole number -- say 3.4% --then convert it to a decimal expressed as hundredths. 3.4 is the same as 3.40 (or 3 and forty hundredths). Now ask yourself how you would express "three and forty hundredths" as a fraction. It would, of course, be 3 40/100. Reduce this and it becomes 3 2/5.

How to Answer Basic Math Multiple Choice

The time allowed on the math portion of a standardized test is typically so short that there's no room for error. You have to be fast and accurate.

Math strategy is very helpful, but nothing beats knowing your stuff! Make sure that you have learned all the important formulas that will be used.

If you don't know the formulas, strategy won't help you.

How to Answer Basic Math Questions - the Basics

First, read the problem, but not the answers.

Work through the problem first and come up with your own answers. Hopefully, you should find your answer among the choices.

If no answer matches the one you got, re-check your math, but this time, use a different method. In math, there are different ways to solve a problem.

Math Multiple Choice Strategy

The two strategies for working with basic math multiple choice are Estimation and Elimination.

Estimation is just as it sounds - try to estimate an approximate answer first. Then look at the choices.

Elimination is probably the most powerful strategy for answering multiple choice.

Eliminate obviously incorrect answers and narrowing the possible choices.

Here are a few basic math examples of how this works.

Solve 2/3 + 5/12

    a. 9/17
    b. 3/11
    c. 7/12
    d. 1 1/12

First estimate the answer. 2/3 is more than half and 5/12 is about half, so the answer is going to be very close to 1.

Next, Eliminate. Choice A is about 1/2 and can be eliminated, choice B is very small, less than 1/2 and can be eliminated. Choice C is close to 1/2 and can be eliminated. Leaving only choice D, which is just over 1.

Work through the solution, find a common denominator and add. The correct answer is 1 1/12, so Choice D is correct.

Let's look at another example:

Solve 4/5 – 2/3

    a. 2/2
    b. 2/13
    c. 1
    d. 2/15

First, quickly estimate the answer. 4/5 is very close to 1, and 2/3 more than half, so the answer is going to be less than 1/2.

Choice A can be eliminated right away, because it is 1. Choice C can be eliminated for the same reason.

Next, look at the denominators. Since 5 and 3 don't go into 13, choice B can be eliminated as well.

That leaves choice D. Checking the answer, the common denominator will be 15. So the answer is 2/15 and choice D is correct.

Fractions shortcut - Cancelling out.

In any operation with fractions, if the numerator of one fraction has a common multiple with the denominator of the other, you can cancel out. This saves time, and simplifies the problem quickly, making it easier to manage.

Solve 2/15 ÷ 4/5

    a. 6/65

    b. 6/75

    c. 5/12

    d. 1/6

To divide fractions, we multiply the first fraction with the inverse of the second fraction. Therefore we have 2/15 x 5/4. The numerator of the first fraction, 2, shares a multiple with the denominator of the second fraction, 4, which is 2. These cancel out, which gives, 1/3 x 1/2 = 1/6

Cancelling Out solved the questions very quickly, but we can still use multiple choice strategies to answer.

Choice B can be eliminated because 75 is too large a denominator. Choice C can be eliminated because 5 and 15 don't go into 12.

Choice D is correct.

Decimal Multiple Choice Strategy and Shortcuts.

Multiplying decimals gives a very quick way to estimate and eliminate choices. Anytime that you multiply decimals, it is going to give an answer with the same number of decimal places as the combined operands.

So for example,

2.38 X 1.2 will produce a number with three places of decimal, which is 2.856.

Here are a few examples with step-by-step explanation:

Solve 2.06 x 1.2

    a. 24.82

    b. 2.482

    c. 24.72

    d. 2.472

This is a simple question, but even before you start calculating, you can eliminate several choices. When multiplying decimals, there will always be as many numbers behind the decimal place in the answer as the sum of the ones in the initial problem, so choices A and C can be eliminated.

The correct answer is D: 2.06 x 1.2 = 2.472

Solve 20.0 ÷ 2.5

    a. 12.05

    b. 9.25

    c. 8.3

    d. 8

First estimate the answer to be around 10, and eliminate choice A. And since it'd also be an even number, you can eliminate Choices B and C, leaving only choice D.

The correct answer is D: 20.0 ÷ 2.5 = 8

TYPES OF WORD PROBLEMS

Word problems can be classified into 12 types. Below are examples of each type with a complete solution. Some types of word problems can be solved quickly using multiple choice strategies and some cannot. Always look for ways to estimate the answer and then eliminate choices.

1. Age

A girl is 10 years older than her brother. By next year, she will be twice the age of her brother. What are their ages now?
    a. 25, 15
    b. 19, 9
    c. 21, 11
    d. 29, 19

Solution: B

We will assume that the girl's age is "a" and her brother's is "b." This means that based on the information in the first sentence,
$a = 10 + b$

Next year, she will be twice her brother's age, which gives
$a + 1 = 2(b + 1)$

We need to solve for one unknown factor and then use the answer to solve for the other. To do this we substitute the value of "a" from the first equation into the second equation. This gives

$10 + b + 1 = 2b + 2$
$11 + b = 2b + 2$
$11 - 2 = 2b - b$
$b = 9$

$9 = b$ this means that her brother is 9 years old. Solving for the girl's age in the first equation gives a = 10 + 9. a = 19 the girl is aged 19. So, the girl is aged 19 and the boy is 9

2. Distance or speed

Two boats travel down a river towards the same destination, starting at the same time. One boat is traveling at 52 km/hr, and the other boat at 43 km/hr. How far apart will they be after 40 minutes?

    a. 46.67 km
    b. 19.23 km
    c. 6 km
    d. 14.39 km

Solution: C

After 40 minutes, the first boat will have traveled = 52 km/hr x 40 minutes/60 minutes = 34.66 km
After 40 minutes, the second boat will have traveled = 43 km/hr x 40/60 minutes = 28.66 km
Difference between the two boats will be 34.66 km – 28.66 km = 6 km.

Multiple Choice Strategy

First estimate the answer. The first boat is traveling 9 km. faster than the second, for 40 minutes, which is 2/3 of an hour. 2/3 of 9 = 6, as a rough guess of the distance apart.

Choices A, B and D can be eliminated right away.

3. Ratio

A recipe states that 700 grams of flour must be mixed in 100 ml of water, and 0.90 grams of salt added. A cook however has just 325 grams of flour. How much water and salt should be used?

    a. 0.41 grams and 46.4 ml
    b. 0.45 grams and 49.3 ml
    c. 0.39 grams and 39.8 ml
    d. 0.25 grams and 40.1 ml

Solution: A

The Cookbook states 700 grams of flour, but the cook only has 325. The first step is to determine the percentage of flour he has 325/700 x 100 = 46.4%
That means that 46.4% of all other items must also be used.
46.4% of 100 = 46.4 ml of water
46.4% of 0.90 = 0.41 grams of salt.

Multiple Choice Strategy

The recipe calls for 700 grams of flour but the cook only has 325, which is just less than half, the quantity of water and salt are going to be about half.

Choices C and D can be eliminated right away. Choice B is very close so be careful. Looking closely at Choice B, it is exactly half, and since 325 is slightly less than half of 700, it can't be correct.

Choice A is correct.

4. Percent

An agent received $6,685 as his commission for selling a property. If his commission was 13% of the selling price, how much was the property?

    a. $68,825
    b. $121,850
    c. $49,025
    d. $51,423

Solution: D

Let's assume that the property price is x
That means from the information given, 13% of x = 6,685
Solve for x,
x = 6685 x 100/13 = $51,423

Multiple Choice Strategy

The commission, 13%, is just over 10%, which is easier to work with. Round up $6685 to $6700, and multiple by 10 for an approximate answer. 10 X 6700 = $67,000. You can do this in your head. Choice B is much too big and can be eliminated. Choice C is too small and can be eliminated. Choices A and D are left and good possibilities.

Do the calculations to make the final choice.

5. Sales & Profit

A store owner buys merchandise for $21,045. He transports them for $3,905 and pays his staff $1,450 to stock the merchandise on his shelves. If he does not incur further costs, how much does he need to sell the items to make $5,000 profit?

    a. $32,500
    b. $29,350
    c. $32,400
    d. $31,400

Solution: D

Total cost of the items is $21,045 + $3,905 + $1,450 = $26,400
Total cost is now $26,400 + $5000 profit = $31,400

Multiple Choice Strategy

Round off and add the numbers up in your head quickly.
21,000 + 4,000 + 1500 = 26500. Add in 5000 profit for a total of 31500.

Choice B is too small and can be eliminated. Choice C and Choice A are too large and can be eliminated.

6. Tax/Income

A woman earns $42,000 per month and pays 5% tax on her monthly income. If the Government increases her monthly taxes by $1,500, what is her income after tax?

    a. $38,400
    b. $36,050
    c. $40,500
    d. $39, 500

Solution: A

Initial tax on income was 5/100 x 42,000 = $2,100
$1,500 was added to the tax to give $2,100 + 1,500 = $3,600
Income after tax left is $42,000 - $3,600 = $38,400

7. Interest

A man invests $3000 in a 2-year term deposit that pays 3% interest per year. How much will he have at the end of the 2-year term?

    a. $5,200
    b. $3,020
    c. $3,182.7
    d. $3,000

Solution: C

This is a compound interest problem. The funds are invested for 2 years and interest is paid yearly, so in the second year, he will earn interest on the interest paid in the first year.
3% interest in the first year = 3/100 x 3,000 = $90
At end of first year, total amount = 3,000 + 90 = $3,090
Second year = 3/100 x 3,090 = 92.7.
At end of second year, total amount = $3090 + $92.7 = $3,182.7

8. Averaging

The average weight of 10 books is 54 grams. 2 more books were added and the average weight became 55.4. If one of the 2 new books added weighed 62.8 g, what is the weight of the other?

    a. 44.7 g

    b. 67.4 g

    c. 62 g

    d. 52 g

Solution: C

Total weight of 10 books with average 54 grams will be = 10 × 54 = 540 g
Total weight of 12 books with average 55.4 will be = 55.4 × 12 = 664.8 g
So total weight of the remaining 2 will be = 664.8 − 540 = 124.8 g
If one weighs 62.8, the weight of the other will be = 124.8 g − 62.8 g = 62 g

Multiple Choice Strategy

Averaging problems can be estimated by looking at which direction the average goes. If additional items are added and the average goes up, the new items much be greater than the average. If the average goes down after new items are added, the new items must be less than the average.
Here, the average is 54 grams and 2 books are added which

increases the average to 55.4, so the new books must weight more than 54 grams.

Choices A and D can be eliminated right away.

9. Probability

A bag contains 15 marbles of various colors. If 3 marbles are white, 5 are red and the rest are black, what is the probability of randomly picking out a black marble from the bag?

    a. 7/15
    b. 3/15
    c. 1/5
    d. 4/15

Solution: A

Total marbles = 15
Number of black marbles = 15 − (3 + 5) = 7
Probability of picking out a black marble = 7/15

10. Two Variables

A company paid a total of $2850 to book for 6 single rooms and 4 double rooms in a hotel for one night. Another company paid $3185 to book for 13 single rooms for one night in the same hotel. What is the cost for single and double rooms in that hotel?

    a. single= $250 and double = $345
    b. single= $254 and double = $350
    c. single = $245 and double = $305
    d. single = $245 and double = $345

Solution: D

We can determine the price of single rooms from the information given of the second company. 13 single rooms = 3185.
One single room = 3185 / 13 = 245
The first company paid for 6 single rooms at $245. 245 x 6 = $1470
Total amount paid for 4 double rooms by first company = $2850 - $1470 = $1380
Cost per double room = 1380 / 4 = $345

11. Geometry

The length of a rectangle is 5 in. more than its width. The perimeter of the rectangle is 26 in. What is the width and length of the rectangle?

    a. width = 6 inches, Length = 9 inches

    b. width = 4 inches, Length = 9 inches

    c. width =4 inches, Length = 5 inches

    d. width = 6 inches, Length = 11 inches

Solution: B

Formula for perimeter of a rectangle is 2(L + W)
p=26, so 2(L + W) = p
The length is 5 inches more than the width, so
2(w + 5) + 2w = 26
2w + 10 + 2w = 26
2w + 2w = 26 - 10
4w = 16

W = 16/4 = 4 inches

L is 5 inches more than w, so L = 5 + 4 = 9 inches.

12. Totals and Fractions

A basket contains 125 oranges, mangoes and apples. If 3/5 of the fruits in the basket are mangoes and only 2/5 of the mangoes are ripe, how many ripe mangoes are there in the basket?

    a. 30
    b. 68
    c. 55
    d. 47

Solution: A
Number of mangoes in the basket is 3/5 x 125 = 75
Number of ripe mangoes = 2/5 x 75 = 30

LOGIC

THIS SECTION CONTAINS A SELF-ASSESSMENT AND LOGIC TUTORIAL. The tutorials are designed to familiarize general principles and the self-assessment contains general questions similar to the logic questions likely to be on the APCAT Entrance Test, but are not intended to be identical to the exam questions. The tutorials are not designed to be a complete logic course, and it is assumed that students have some familiarity with logic questions. If you do not understand parts of the tutorial, or find the tutorial difficult, it is recommended that you seek out additional instruction.

Tour of the APCAT Test Logic

The APCAT logic section has 20 questions. Below is a detailed list of the types of logic questions that generally appear on the APCAT test.

- Ordering information in a logical sequence
- Solving problems
- Identifying patterns in data

The questions below are not the same as you will find on the APCAT test- that would be too easy! And nobody knows what the questions will be and they change all the time. Mostly the changes consist of substituting new questions for old, but the changes can be new question formats or styles, changes to the number of questions in each section, changes to the time limits for each section and combining sections. Below are general logic questions that cover the same areas and are intended for skill practice. While the format and exact wording of the questions may differ slightly, and change from year to year, if you can answer the questions below, you will have no problem with the logic section of the APCAT test.

Logic Self-Assessment

The purpose of the self-assessment is:

- Identify your strengths and weaknesses.
- Develop your personalized study plan (above)
- Get accustomed to the APCAT Entrance test format
- Extra practice – the self-assessments are almost a full 3rd practice test!
- Provide a baseline score for preparing your study schedule.

Since this is a Self-assessment, and depending on how confident you are with logic and problem solving, timing is optional. The APCAT has 20 logic questions. The self-assessment has 10 questions, so allow about 10 minutes to complete.

Once complete, use the table below to assess your understanding of the content, and prepare your study schedule described in chapter 1.

80% - 100%	Excellent – you have mastered the content
60 – 79%	Good. You have a working knowledge. Even though you can just pass this section, you may want to review the tutorials and do some extra practice to see if you can improve your mark.
40% - 59%	Below Average. You do not understand verbal skills problems. Review the tutorials, and retake this quiz again in a few days, before proceeding to the Practice Test Questions.
Less than 40%	Poor. You have a very limited understanding of verbal skills problems. Please review the tutorials, and retake this quiz again in a few days, before proceeding to the Practice Test Questions.

Logic Answer Sheet

	A	B	C	D
1	○	○	○	○
2	○	○	○	○
3	○	○	○	○
4	○	○	○	○
5	○	○	○	○
6	○	○	○	○
7	○	○	○	○
8	○	○	○	○
9	○	○	○	○
10	○	○	○	○

Number Series

1. Consider the following series: 6, 12, 24, 48. What number should come next?

    a. 48
    b. 64
    c. 60
    d. 96

2. Consider the following series: 5, 6, 11, 17. What number should come next?

    a. 28
    b. 34
    c. 36
    d. 27

3. Consider the following series: 26, 21, ..., 11, 6. What is the missing number?

    a. 27
    b. 23
    c. 16
    d. 29

4. Consider the following series: 23, ..., 31, 37. What is the missing number?

    a. 19
    b. 27
    c. 29
    d. 30

Directions: Find the sentence that is true according to the given information.

5. Krizzia loves reading books. Nea enjoys playing with her dolls. Krizzia and Nea are cousins.

    a. Krizzia likes to play with Nea.

    b. Nea finds reading boring.

    c. Krizzia and Nea are blood related

    d. Nea and Krizzia are best friends.

6. The village is found in a coastal area. Many fishermen go out to sea everyday. They go home late in the afternoon.

    a. Fishing is the means of living of the villagers.

    b. Many fishermen hate fishing.

    c. Fishermen go out to sea especially in the evening.

    d. The village attracts tourists.

Question 7 is based on the following information.

7. Five billboards appear on a highway. They are numbered from 1 to 5, starting at 1, and proceeding up to 5 as you drive by.

    a. The first billboard is for Lasik eye surgery.

    b. A Vietnamese restaurant is 2nd.

    c. There are 3 billboards between the Lasik Eye surgery billboard and the McDonalds' Billboard.

    d. There is one billboard before the Life Insurance billboard.

What position is the Wells Fargo Billboard?

   a. Second

   b. Third

   c. Fourth

   d. Cannot be determined.

8. Place the following four sentences in logical order.

   1. Interview suspect who claims he isn't married

   2. Called to domestic dispute

   3. Suspect flees on foot and is apprehended

   4. Computer search reveals a man matching the suspects description is the husband of the woman making the complaint

   a. 2, 3, 1, 4

   b. 4, 2, 3, 1

   c. 3, 2, 1, 4

   d. The order is correct

You are interviewing a woman who has been assaulted walking home from the bus stop. You ask her to re-trace her steps from the bus stop.

She got off the bus on Victoria Ave. and walked to Birch st., where she turned right. She walked along Birch St. and turned right on Elm St. She first noticed that she was being followed on Elm. She continued walking on Elm and turned left on Maple St. Her assailant tried to grab her purse on Maple St. She escaped and ran down Maple, turning left on Spruce, where she ran north to her house.

9. What direction was she traveling on Elm?

    a. North

    b. South

    c. East

    d. West

10. What direction was she traveling when she noticed she was attacked?

    a. North

    b. South

    c. East

    d. West

Answer Key

Section I - Number Series

1. D
The numbers double each time.

2. A
Each number is the sum of the previous two numbers.

3. C
The numbers decrease by 5 each time.

4. C
The numbers are primes (divisible only by 1 and themselves).

5. C
The only certain thing is Krizzia and Nea are related to each other.

6. A
The only certain thing is the villagers rely on fishing to earn money since they live near the ocean.

7. B
Lasik is #1. The Vietnamese restaurant is #2, and there is 1 before the Life Insurance, so Life Insurance must be 4th. There are 3 billboards between Lasik and McDonalds, so Lasik and McDonalds must be first and last. The only position left for Wells Fargo is #3.

    1 Lasik Eye Surgery
    2 - Vietnamese Restaurant
    3 -
    4 - Life Insurance
    5 - McDonalds

8. A
2, 3, 1, 4

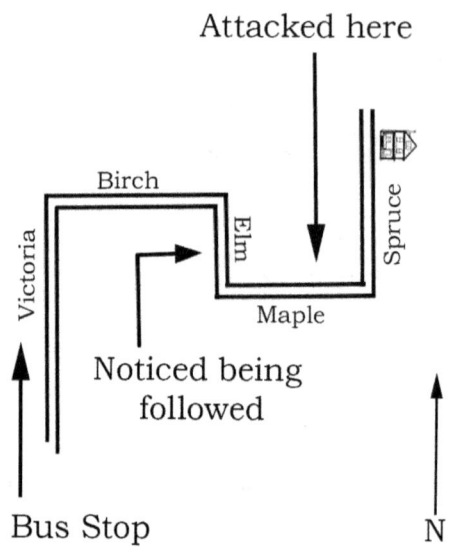

9. B
She was traveling South on Elm.

10. C
She was traveling East on Maple when she was attacked.

Number Series Tutorial

Number series questions appear on most High School exams. An example is:
Consider the following series: 26, 21, 0, 11, 6. What is the missing number?

    a. 27
    b. 23
    c. 16
    d. 29

Looking carefully at the sequence, we can see right away that each number is 5 less than the previous number, so the missing number is 16.

We can re-write this sequence in mathematical notation as, $a_1, a_2, a_3, \ldots a_n$, where n is an integer and an is called its nth term. And we can write the sequence in the form of a formula, where an integer is substituted in the place of the variable in the formula and the terms are obtained.

For example, let us consider the sequence 5,10,15,20,...

- Here, $a_n = 5n$. The formula $a_n = 5n$.
- The nth term of a sequence can be found by plugging n in the explicit formula for the sequence. So for example if we wanted to find the 100th number in this sequence, we would substitute n = 100 in the formula and get 500.

Type of Number Sequence Problems

1. Simple addition or subtraction – each number in the sequence is obtained by adding a number to the previous number.

For example, 2, 5, 8, 11, 14

Each number in the sequence is obtained by adding 3 to the previous number, which we could write as, $a_{n+1} = a_n + 3$.

2. Simple multiplication - each number in the sequence is obtained by multiplying the previous number by a whole number or fraction.

For example, 3, 6, 18, 54

Or,

20, 10, 5, 2.5

Each number in the first sequence is obtained by multiplying the previous number by 3, which we could write as, $a_{n+1} = a_n \times 3$.

In the second example, each number in the series is the previous number divided by 2, or multiplied by 1/2, or $a_{n+1} = a_n \times 1/2$.

3. Prime Numbers – each number in the sequence is a prime number.

For example,

23, ..., 31, 37

Answer: 29

4. Operations on the previous two numbers. For example,

8, 14, 22, 36, 58

Here the sequence is created by adding the previous 2 numbers.

5. Exponents. The number sequence is created by each number squared or cubed.

For example,

3, 9, 81, 6561, where each number is squared.

6. Combining Sequences

2, 7, 13, 20, 28, 37

Here the sequence starts with 2, and each element is added to another sequence starting with 5. So, 2 + 5 = 7, 7 + 6 = 13, 13 + 7 = 20 and so on.

A variation is a sequence with a repeating element. For example,

1, 2, 3, 5, 7, 9, 12, 15

Here the sequence is, for each n, +1, +1, +1, +2, +2, +2, +3, +3,

7. Fractions

For example,

16/4, 4/2, 2/2, ½, 0
Fractions are often meant to confuse. If fractions don't have an obvious relationship, reduce them to lowest terms or to whole numbers. Reducing these to whole numbers, gives,

4, 2, 1, ½

Right away, we can see the numbers are half the previous number, so the next in the series is 1/4.

In this example, the answer is a fraction; however, you may have to reduce fractions to see the relation, and then convert back to get the answer in the correct form.

Strategy for Answering Number Series Questions

Answering number series questions is a skill of recognizing patterns, and the best way to improve is to familiarize yourself with the different types, and to practice.

Here is a quick method that will help you answer number series.

For example:

2, 5, 6, 7, 8, ...

Step 1 – glance at the series quickly and see if you can spot the pattern right away.

Step 2 – Start analyzing.

Take the different between the first 2 numbers and the different between the second 2 numbers.

2, (+3) 5, (+1)   6, (+1) 7, (+1)   8,

No clear pattern with a simple analysis. There is no addition, subtraction, multiplication, division, fractional or exponent relationship.

The relation must be a higher order or a second series.

Next look at the relation between the 1st number and the 2nd and the 1st and the 3rd. We see that,
1st + 3 = 5, 1st + 4 = 6. That's it! The number 2 is added to the sequence, 3, 4, 5, 6, so the next number will be 2 + 7 = 9.

Logic Tutorial

https://www.test-preparation.ca/logic-tutorial/

Practice Test Questions Set 1

THE QUESTIONS BELOW ARE NOT THE SAME AS YOU WILL FIND ON THE APCAT ENTRANCE TEST- THAT WOULD BE TOO EASY! And nobody knows what the questions will be and they change all the time. Below are general questions that cover the same subject areas as the APCAT Entrance Test. So, while the format and exact wording of the questions may differ slightly, and change from year to year, if you can answer the questions below, you will have no problem with the APCAT Test.

For the best results, take these practice test questions as if it were the real exam. Set aside time when you will not be disturbed, and a location that is quiet and free of distractions. Read the instructions carefully, read each question carefully, and answer to the best of your ability.

Use the bubble answer sheets provided. When you have completed the practice questions, check your answer against the Answer Key and read the explanation provided.

Do not attempt more than one set of practice test questions in one day. After completing the first practice test, wait two or three days before attempting the second set of questions.

Observation – 7 Questions

Professional Judgment: 10 Questions

Recognition/Identification – 3 Questions

ACT – 20 questions

Math - 20 questions

Logic – 20 questions

Observation

```
   A B C D
1  ○ ○ ○ ○
2  ○ ○ ○ ○
3  ○ ○ ○ ○
4  ○ ○ ○ ○
5  ○ ○ ○ ○
6  ○ ○ ○ ○
7  ○ ○ ○ ○
```

Judgment and Recognition

	A	B	C	D
1	○	○	○	○
2	○	○	○	○
3	○	○	○	○
4	○	○	○	○
5	○	○	○	○
6	○	○	○	○
7	○	○	○	○
8	○	○	○	○
9	○	○	○	○
10	○	○	○	○
11	○	○	○	○
12	○	○	○	○
13	○	○	○	○

ACT

	A	B	C	D
1	○	○	○	○
2	○	○	○	○
3	○	○	○	○
4	○	○	○	○
5	○	○	○	○
6	○	○	○	○
7	○	○	○	○
8	○	○	○	○
9	○	○	○	○
10	○	○	○	○
11	○	○	○	○
12	○	○	○	○
13	○	○	○	○
14	○	○	○	○
15	○	○	○	○
16	○	○	○	○
17	○	○	○	○
18	○	○	○	○
19	○	○	○	○
20	○	○	○	○

Mathematics

	A	B	C	D
1	○	○	○	○
2	○	○	○	○
3	○	○	○	○
4	○	○	○	○
5	○	○	○	○
6	○	○	○	○
7	○	○	○	○
8	○	○	○	○
9	○	○	○	○
10	○	○	○	○
11	○	○	○	○
12	○	○	○	○
13	○	○	○	○
14	○	○	○	○
15	○	○	○	○
16	○	○	○	○
17	○	○	○	○
18	○	○	○	○
19	○	○	○	○
20	○	○	○	○

Logic

	A	B	C	D
1	○	○	○	○
2	○	○	○	○
3	○	○	○	○
4	○	○	○	○
5	○	○	○	○
6	○	○	○	○
7	○	○	○	○
8	○	○	○	○
9	○	○	○	○
10	○	○	○	○
11	○	○	○	○
12	○	○	○	○
13	○	○	○	○
14	○	○	○	○
15	○	○	○	○
16	○	○	○	○
17	○	○	○	○
18	○	○	○	○
19	○	○	○	○
20	○	○	○	○

Professional Judgment

Scenario I

You and your partner arrive on a domestic scene where an enraged and possibly drunk or high man is destroying the furniture in a house. His wife or girlfriend is crying nearby.

1. What should you do first?

    a. Subdue the man and then report to dispatch

    b. Report to dispatch and call for backup

    c. Make sure the wife is OK

    d. Check the wife first, then subdue the man

You have confirmed the girlfriend is OK and subdued and placed the man under arrest. He has calmed down. You and your partner are preparing to take the man to the station. He begs you to release him saying it was all a big misunderstanding.

2. What should you do now?

    a. Release the man if he agrees to appear in court.

    b. Take the man to the station.

    c. Discuss what to do with your partner.

    d. Ask dispatch what to do.

Scenario II

You attend a fight in a parking lot near a popular nightclub that has just closed. You and your partner find one man with a bloody nose and looking poorly, and another man who appears to be fine. There is a crowd watching the fight.

3. What should you do?

    a. Check the injured man, keeping the men separate.

    b. Arrest both men

    c. Arrest both men and interview them separately.

    d. Check the injured man, interview both men separately.

Scenario III

4. You have just arrested a man for breaking and entering. You apprehended the suspect inside a residence with broken windows. The man tells you he will give you the name of 2 other people who recently robbed a bank in your patrol area if you let him go.

What should you do?

    a. Take down the information and let him go.

    b. Take down the information and continue with the arrest and processing.

    c. Tell him he will have to give you information about 2 or more crimes before you can let him go

    d. Call dispatch for advice.

Scenario IV

5. You have pulled over a vehicle for dangerous driving and arrested the driver. The driver of the vehicle has agreed to accompany you to the station. The driver has requested he drive his own vehicle behind yours.

What should you do?

>   a. You determine the driver has not been drinking and appears calm, so you allow the driver to follow you to the station.
>
>   b. Refuse his request and ask dispatch to call a tow truck.
>
>   c. Question the driver more before allowing him to drive back
>
>   d. Allow the suspect to drive his own car back with some restrictions.

Scenario V

6. You attend a call to a beach party. Nearby some cars have been vandalized. It is not clear if the people at the beach party are responsible or not, and they deny vandalizing the cars. There are 8 or 10 people at the beach party and they appear peaceful.

What should you do?

>   a. Call for backup before approaching the beach party.
>
>   b. Approach the beach party and ask if they know about the vandalized cars.
>
>   c. Arrest everyone at the beach party.
>
>   d. Take the names of everyone at the party.

7. Backup has arrived and you approach the beach party with 2 other officers. You are the senior officer at the scene.

What is your next step?

    a. Arrest everyone at the party

    b. Question everyone at the party about the vandalized cars

    c. Accuse everyone at the party of vandalizing the cars to see their reaction

    d. Examine the vandalized cars with the other officers.

Scenario VI

8. You have pulled over a car for speeding and are about to write up a ticket. The driver tells you he knows the mayor and the chief of police and will get you fired if you give him a ticket. He asked for your name and badge number.

What should you do?

    a. Refuse to give your name or badge.

    b. Give the driver a warning instead of a ticket

    c. Let the driver go

    d. Give your name and badge number and give him a ticket.

Scenario VII

You have attended a domestic violence call. The woman has clearly been beaten by the man, and when you enter the house, the man is breaking china and furniture.

9. What should you do first?

    a. Stop the man from further property damage.

    b. Attend the woman's injuries

    c. Call for backup

d. Check the house for other people or children.

Scenario VIII

You are called to a robbery at a jewelry store. You arrive and the owner of the store is unconscious and the a male is exiting the store by the front door as you enter the back. The male robbery suspect is carrying a bag, which may contain jewelry from the store.

10. What should you do?

    a. Chase the robbery suspect.

    b. Check the unconscious owner

    c. Assess what has been stolen

    d. Call for backup

Recognition and Identification

11. Choose the person that matches the suspect below.

a.

b.

c.

d.

12. Choose the person that matches the suspect below.

a.

b.

c.

d.

13. Choose the person that matches the suspect below.

a.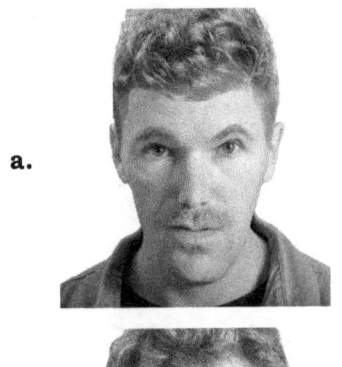

b.

c.

d.

Alberta Communications Test

1. Choose a verb that means fearless or invulnerable to intimidation and fear.

    a. Feeble

    b. Strongest

    c. Dauntless

    d. Super

2. Choose a word that means the same as the underlined word.

I see the differences when they are placed side-by-side and <u>juxtaposed.</u>

    a. Compared

    b. Eliminated

    c. Overturned

    d. Exonerated

3. Choose the best definition of regicide.

    a. v. To endow or furnish with requisite ability, character, knowledge and skill

    b. n. killing of a king

    c. adj. Disposed to seize by violence or by unlawful or greedy methods

    d. v. To refresh after labor

4. Choose the best definition of pernicious.

    a. Deadly

    b. Infectious

    c. Common

    d. Rare

5. Fill in the blank.

After she received her influenza vaccination, Nan thought that she was _____ to the common cold.

    a. Immune

    b. Susceptible

    c. Vulnerable

    d. At risk

6. Choose a word that means the same as the underlined word.

She performed the gymnastics and stretches so well! I have never seen anyone so <u>nimble</u>.

    a. Awkward

    b. Agile

    c. Quick

    d. Taut

7. Choose a word that means the same as the underlined word.

Are there any more <u>queries</u>? We have already had so many questions today.

    a. Questions

    b. Commands

    c. Obfuscations

    d. Paradoxes

8. Choose a verb that means to remove a leader or high official from position.

    a. Sack

    b. Suspend

    c. Depose

    d. Dropped

9. Choose the best definition of pedestrian.

   a. Rare
   b. Often
   c. Walking or Running
   d. Commonplace

10. Choose the best definition of petulant.

   a. Patient
   b. Childish
   c. Impatient
   d. Mature

11. Choose the correct spelling.

   a. Humoros
   b. Humouros
   c. Humorous
   d. Humorus

12. Choose the correct spelling.

   a. Knowlege
   b. Knowledge
   c. Knowlegde
   d. Knowlledge

13. Choose the correct spelling.

   a. Camaraderie
   b. Camaredere
   c. Camaradere
   d. Cameraderie

14. Choose the correct spelling.

a. Mathematics
b. Mathmatics
c. Matematics
d. Mathamatics

15. Choose the correct spelling.

a. Conscentious
b. Conscientios
c. Conscientious
d. Consceintious

16. Choose the correct spelling.

a. Leisuire
b. Lesure
c. Lesure
d. Leisure

17. Choose the correct spelling.

a. Pigeone
b. Pigoen
c. Pigeon
d. Pidgeon

18. Choose the correct spelling.

a. Odyessy
b. Odeyssey
c. Odysey
d. Odyssey

19. Choose the correct spelling.

    a. Sacreligious

    b. Sacriligious

    c. Sacrilegious

    d. Sacrilegous

20. Choose the correct spelling.

    a. Accommodate

    b. Accommodate

    c. Acommodate

    d. Accommodaite

21. Choose the sentence with the correct capitalization.

    a. My favorite Dylan song is blowin' in the wind.

    b. My favorite dylan song is Blowin' in the Wind.

    c. My favorite Dylan song is Blowin' in the Wind.

    d. None of the above.

22. Choose the sentence with the correct capitalization.

    a. My latest novel, Danger on the Rhine will be published next year.

    b. My latest novel, danger on the Rhine will be published next year.

    c. My latest novel, danger on the rhine will be published next year.

    d. None of the above.

23. Choose the sentence with the correct usage.

a. The Chinese live in one of the world's most populous nations, while a citizen of Bermuda lives in one of the least populous.

b. The Chinese lives in one of the world's most populous nations, while a citizen of Bermuda live in one of the least populous.

c. The Chinese live in one of the world's most populous nations, while a citizen of Bermuda live in one of the least populous.

d. The Chinese lives in one of the world's most populous nations, while a citizen of Bermuda lives in one of the least populous.

24. Choose the sentence with the correct usage.

a. Disease is highly prevalent in poorer nations; the most dominant disease is malaria.

b. Diseases are highly prevalent in poorer nations; the most dominant disease is malaria.

c. Disease is highly prevalent in poorer nations; the most dominant Diseases are malaria.

d. Diseases are highly prevalent in poorer nations; the most dominant Diseases are malaria.

25. Choose the sentence with the correct usage.

a. Although I would prefer to have dog, I actually own a cat.

b. Although I would prefer to have a dog, I actually own cat.

c. Although I would prefer to have a dog, I actually own a cat.

d. Although I would prefer to have dog, I actually own cat.

26. Choose the sentence with the correct usage.

a. The volunteers brought groceries and toys to the homeless shelter; the latter were given to the staff, while the former were given directly to the children.

b. The volunteers brought groceries and toys to the homeless shelter; the former was given to the staff, while the latter was given directly to the children.

c. The volunteers brought groceries and toys to the homeless shelter; the groceries were given to the staff, while the former was given directly to the children.

d. The volunteers brought groceries and toys to the homeless shelter; the latter was given to the staff, while the groceries were given directly to the children.

27. Choose the sentence with the correct grammar.

a. His doctor suggested that he eat less snacks and do fewer lounging on the couch.

b. His doctor suggested that he eat fewer snacks and do less lounging on the couch.

c. His doctor suggested that he eat less snacks and do less lounging on the couch.

d. His doctor suggested that he eat fewer snacks and do fewer lounging on the couch.

28. Choose the sentence with the correct grammar.

a. However, I believe that he didn't really try that hard.
b. However I believe that he didn't really try that hard.
c. However; I believe that he didn't really try that hard.
d. However: I believe that he didn't really try that hard.

29. Choose the sentence with the correct grammar.

a. There was however, very little difference between the two.

b. There was, however very little difference between the two.

c. There was; however, very little difference between the two.

d. There was, however, very little difference between the two.

30. Choose the sentence with the correct grammar.

a. Don would never have thought of that book, but you could have reminded him.

b. Don would never of thought of that book, but you could have reminded him.

c. Don would never have thought of that book, but you could of have reminded him.

d. Don would never of thought of that book, but you could of reminded him.

MATHEMATICS

1. What is 1/3 of 3/4?

    a. 1/4
    b. 1/3
    c. 2/3
    d. 3/4

2. What fraction of $1500 is $75?

    a. 1/14
    b. 3/5
    c. 7/10
    d. 1/20

3. 3.14 + 2.73 + 23.7 =

    a. 28.57
    b. 30.57
    c. 29.56
    d. 29.57

4. A woman spent 15% of her income on an item and ends with $120. What percentage of her income is left?

    a. 12%
    b. 85%
    c. 75%
    d. 95%

5. A mother is making spaghetti for her son. The recipe that she's using says that for 500 grams of spaghetti, she should add 0.75 grams of salt. However, the mom just wants 125 grams of spaghetti. Based on this information, how much salt should she use?

    a. 0.38 grams
    b. 0.75 grams
    c. 0.19 grams
    d. 0.25 grams

6. A pet store sold $19,304.56 worth of merchandise in June. If the cost of products sold was $5,284.34, employees were paid $8,384.76, and rent was $2,920.00, how much profit did the store make in June?

    a. $5,635.46
    b. $2,715.46
    c. $14,020.22
    d. $10,019.80

7. At the beginning of 2009, Madalyn invested $5,000 in a savings account. The account pays 4% interest per year. At the end of the year, after the interest was awarded, how much did Madalyn have in the account?

   a. $5,200
   b. $5,020
   c. $5,110
   d. $7,000

8. If 144 students need to go on a trip and the buses each carry 36 students, how many buses are needed?

   a. 6
   b. 5
   c. 4
   d. 3

9. If a square if five feet tall, what is its area?

   a. 5 square feet
   b. 10 square feet
   c. 20 square feet
   d. 25 square feet

10. With a purely random guess, what are the chances of correctly guessing the month in which a person was born?

   a. 1 : 3
   b. 1 : 6
   c. 1 : 4
   d. 1 : 12

11. John is a barber and receives 40% of the amount paid by each of his customers. John gets all tips paid to him. If a man pays $8.50 for a haircut and pays a tip of $1.30, how much money goes to John?

    a. $3.92
    b. $4.70
    c. $5.30
    d. $6.40

12. Susan was surprised to find she had two more quarters than she believed she had in her purse. If quarters are the only coins, and the total is $8.75, how many quarters did she think she had?

    a. 35
    b. 29
    c. 31
    d. 33

13. There were some oranges in a basket, by adding 8/5 of these, the total became 130. How many oranges were in the basket?

    a. 60
    b. 50
    c. 40
    d. 35

14. Mr. Brown bought 5 burgers, 3 drinks, 4 fries for his family and a cookie for the dog. If the price of all single items is same, at $1.30 and a 3.5% tax is added, then what is the total cost of dinner?

    a. $16.00
    b. $16.90
    c. $17.00
    d. $17.50

15. A distributor purchased 550 kilograms of potatoes for $165. He distributed these at a rate of $6.4 per 20 kilograms to 15 shops, $3.4 per 10 kilograms to 12 shops and the remainder at $1.8 per 5 kilograms. If his total distribution cost is $10, what will his profit be?

    a. $10.40
    b. $8.60
    c. $14.90
    d. $23.40

16. Convert 3 yards to feet

    a. 18 feet
    b. 12 feet
    c. 9 feet
    d. 27 feet

17. 12t - 10 = 14t + 2. Find t

    a. -6
    b. -4
    c. 4
    d. 6

18. The price of a book went up from $20 to $25. What percent did the price increase?

    a. 5%
    b. 10%
    c. 20%
    d. 25%

19. The price of a book decreased from $25 to $20. What percent did the price decrease?

    a. 5%

    b. 10%

    c. 20%

    d. 25%

20. 305 X 25 =

    a. 6525

    b. 7625

    c. 5026

    d. 7026

Part IV - Logic

1. Consider the following sequence: 13, 26, 52, 104, ... What number should come next?

    a. 208

    b. 106

    c. 200

    d. 400

2. Consider the following sequence: 32, 26, 20, 14, ... What number should come next?

    a. 12

    b. 19

    c. 10

    d. 8

3. Consider the following sequence: 12, 4, 16, ..., 36. What is the missing number?

    a. 18

    b. 22

    c. 20

    d. 30

Directions: Find the sentence that is true according to the given information.

4. Ben and Ted are classmates. They would ride the school bus together. They also have lunch at the same table. They're even lab partners.

    a. Ben and Ted don't like each other.

    b. Ben prefers being with other children.

    c. Ben and Ted are inseparable.

    d. Ted is always alone.

5. Karen takes care of her garden everyday. She grows fruits and vegetables. She always waters them. She also pulls out the weeds and put fertilizer on her plants.

    a. Karen hates taking care of her plants.

    b. Karen is fond of gardening.

    c. Karen plants flowers in her garden.

    d. Karen and her mother work on the garden together.

6. Collecting stamps is Tom's hobby. He started collecting stamps when he was six years old. Today, Tom has over a thousand stamps in his collection.

    a. Tom collects stamp albums.

    b. Tom started collecting stamps in high school.

    c. Tom is a stamp collector.

    d. Collecting stamps is an expensive hobby.

7. Mother went to market. She bought apples, oranges, and bananas. She also bought cabbage, beans, and squash.

    a. Vegetables in the market are expensive.

    b. Mother bought chicken and meat.

    c. Many people went to the market.

    d. Mother bought fruits and vegetables.

8. Tommy and Timmy are brothers. They look the same. They also have the same birthdays.

    a. Tommy is older than Timmy.

    b. Timmy is more handsome than Tommy.

    c. Tommy and Timmy are twins.

    d. Tommy and Timmy are best friends.

9. Five students exam marks are posted on a sheet at the front of the class, from lowest at the top, to highest at the bottom.

1. Peter's mark is smaller than Brad's but higher than Emily's mark.
2. Brad's mark is lower that Brittany's.
3. Andrew's mark is third.

Who got the highest mark?

    a. Emily

    b. Brad

    c. Brittany

    d. Cannot be determined.

In the code below, the following rules apply:

1. Each letter always represents the same word.
2. Each word is represented by only one letter.
3. The position of a letter and a word in the sentence are never the same.

Z	B	W	O	V	means
Linda	likes	French	lessons	best	

B	C	O	V	E	means
Peter	likes	science	lessons	best	

V	A	G	W	N	means
Linda	does	not	like	algebra	

10. What letter represents Linda?

    a. Z
    b. B
    c. W
    d. None of the above.

11. What does 'V' represent?

    a. Science
    b. Lessons
    c. Best
    d. Like

Directions: Read the following report and answer questions 12 and 13.

You come on an accident scene on Majestic Ave. A vehicle has been hit and another vehicle, with a damaged front end is fleeing the scene. The vehicle proceeds north on Majestic and turns right on Arbutus St., then left on Oak st., right on Richmond, and then right again on Birch. The vehicle stops on Birch.

12. What direction was the vehicle traveling on Arbutus?

    a. North
    b. South
    c. East
    d. West

13. What direction was the vehicle traveling on Richmond?

    a. North
    b. South
    c. East
    d. West

14. Arrange the following in the correct sequence.

a. Teens refuse to give their names
b. Several teens flee the scene
c. Dispatch reports a beach party
d. You approach a group of teens

    a. CDAB

    b. DABC

    c. ABCD

    d. ADCB

15. Arrange the following in the correct sequence.

a. Robert Smith is charged.
b. A suspect gives his name as Andrew Jones and is released.
c. The suspect is later arrested by other officers.
d. A records check reveals a person fitting his description is actually Robert Smith with a lengthy list of priors.

    a. ABCD

    b. DCBA

    c. CBDA

    d. BDCA

Answer Key

Professional Judgment

1. D
The priority is safety, so checking the wife is the first thing, then subdue the man.

2. B
There is no reason to release the man as he has caused significant damage.

3. D
The first priority is the ensure safety, then to interview both men separately.

4. B
If the suspect is willing to provide information about another crime, then take the information, but this cannot be bartered for release after arrest.

5. B
Under no circumstances should the suspect drive his own car.

6. A
The safest course of action is the wait for backup.

7. B
The safest action is the approach the beach party and ask if they know anything about the vandalized cars, and your next response will depend on their reaction and information.

8. D
Give your name and badge number and give him a ticket.

9. B
The first objective is to assess the woman's injuries and call for an ambulance if necessary.

10. B
The first responsibility is to the unconscious owner. After, or while assessing the unconscious owner, call update dispatch of the whole situation.

RECOGNITION AND IDENTIFICATION

11. A
Choice A has the same face but different hair. The other suspects have much thinner, or different shaped faces.
12. C
Choice C is the same person wearing sunglasses. The suspect's face in choices A and D are much thinner and the suspect in choice B is wider.

13. C
The suspects in choices A and B have a thinner face, and the suspect in choice D has a wider face.

ALBERTA COMMUNICATIONS TEST

1. C
Dauntless: adj. Invulnerable to fear or intimidation.

2. A
Juxtaposed: adj. Placed side-by-side, often for comparison or contrast.
3. B
Regicide: v. killing of a king.

4. A
Pernicious: adj. Causing much harm in a subtle way.
5. A
Immune: adj. Resistant to a particular infection or toxin owing to the presence of specific antibodies.

6. B
Nimble: adj. Quick and light in movement or action. Agile.

7. A
Queries: n. Questions or inquiries.

8. C
Depose: To remove (a leader) from (high) office, without killing the incumbent.

9. D
Pedestrian: Ordinary, dull; everyday; unexceptional.

10. B
Petulant: adj. Childishly irritable.

11. C
Humorous is the correct spelling.

12. B
Knowledge is the correct spelling.

13. A
Camaraderie is the correct spelling.

14. A
Mathematics is the correct spelling.

15. C
Conscientious is the correct spelling.

16. D
Leisure is the correct spelling.

17. C
Pigeon is the correct spelling.

18. D
Odyssey is the correct spelling.

19. C
Sacrilegious is the correct spelling.

20. A
Accommodate is the correct spelling.

21. C
The major words in the titles of books, articles, and songs are capitalized. (but not short prepositions or the articles "the," "a," or "an," if they are not the first word of the title)

22. A
Titles of publications are capitalized.

23. A
Singular subjects. "The Chinese" is plural, and "a citizen of Bermuda" is singular.

24. A
Disease is singular.

25. C
Articles of speech. Both dog and cat in this sentence are singular and require the article 'a.'

26. B
Former vs. Latter. 'Former' refers to the first of two things, 'latter' to the second.

27. B
Fewer vs. Less. 'Fewer' is used with countables and 'less' is used with un-countables.

28. A
'However' usage. 'However' usually has a comma before and after.

29. D
'However' Usage. 'However' usually has a comma before and after.

30. A
The third conditional is used for talking about an unreal situation (that did not happen) in the past. For example, "If I had studied harder, [if clause] I would have passed the exam [main clause]. Which is the same as, "I failed the exam, because I didn't study hard enough."

Mathematics

1. A
1/3 X 3/4 = 3/12 = 1/4

2. D
75/1500 = 15/300 = 3/60 = 1/20

3. D
3.14 + 2.73 = 5.87 and 5.87 + 23.7 = 29.57

4. B
Spent 15% - 100% - 15% = 85%

5. C
125 : 500 is the same as 25 : 100 or 1 : 4. So the amount of salt will be 0.75/4 = 0.1875, or about .19 grams.

6. B
Total expenses = 5284.34 + $8,384.76 + $2,920.00 = $16,589.10

Profit = revenue less expenses

$19,304.56 - 16589.10 = $2,715.46

7. A
$5,000 at 4% = 5000 X 4/100
5000 X .4 = 200
So the total after one year will be $5,200

8. C
If each bus carries 36 students, and there are 144 students total, then 144/36 = 4 buses.

9. D
If a square is 5 feet tall, then the area will be 5 X 5 = 25.

10. D
Since there are 12 months in a year = 12 possibilities, the chance of guessing the correct month will be 1 in 12.

11. B
John's total will be 40% of 8.50 plus the tip of $1.30.

8.5 X 4/100 = 8.5 X .4 = 3.40

Total = 3.40 + 1.30 = $4.70.

12. D
If she has $8.75, that will equal 35 quarters. ($8.00 = 32 quarters and $.75 = 3 quarters, total 35 quarters).

She had 2 more quarters than she thought, so she had 35 - 2 = 33 quarters.

13. B
Suppose oranges in the basket before = x, Then: X + 8x/5 = 130, 5x + 8x = 650, so X = 50.

14. D
As price of all the single items is same and there are 13 total items. So the total cost will be 13 × 1.3 = $16.90. After 3.5 percent tax this amount will become 16.9×1.035=$17.50.

15. B
The distribution is at three different rates and amounts:

$6.4 per 20 kilograms to 15 shops ... 20•15 = 300 kilograms distributed

$3.4 per 10 kilograms to 12 shops ... 10•12 = 120 kilograms distributed

550 - (300 + 120) = 550 - 420 = 130 kilograms left. This amount is distributed in 5 kilogram portions. So, this means that there are 130/5 = 26 shops.

$1.8 per 130 kilograms.

We need to find the amount he earned overall these distributions.

$6.4 per 20 kilograms : 6.4•15 = $96 for 300 kilograms

$3.4 per 10 kilograms : 3.4•12 = $40.8 for 120 kilograms

$1.8 per 5 kilograms : 1.8•26 = $46.8 for 130 kilograms

So, he earned 96 + 40.8 + 46.8 = $ 183.6

The total cost of distribution is given as $10

The profit is found by: Money earned - money spent ... It is important to remember that he bought 550 kilograms of potatoes for $165 at the beginning:

Profit = 183.6 - 10 - 165 = $8.6

16. C
1 yard = 3 feet, 3 yards = 3 feet x 3 = 9 feet

17. C
12t -10 = 14t + 2

Collect terms with the same variable on the same side, switching to negative if you bring terms over the equals sign.

-2t - 10 = 2

Collect number on the same side switching to negative if you bring terms over the equals sign.

-2t = -8

Divide both sides by -2.
-t = -4
t = 4

18. D
The price increased by $5 ($25-$20). The percent increase is 5/20 x 100 = 5 x 5 = 25%

19. C
The price decreased by $5 ($25-$20). The percent increase = 5/25 x 100 = 5 x 4 = 20%

20. B
305 X 25 = 7625

Logic

1. A
The number doubles each time.

2. D
The numbers decrease by 6 each time.

3. C
Each number is the sum of the previous two numbers.

4. C
The only certain thing is Ben and Ted are inseparable.

5. B
The only certain thing is Karen is fond of gardening.

6. C
The only certain thing is Tom is a stamp collector.

7. D
The only certain thing is mother bought fruits and vegetables.

8. C
The only certain thing is they are twins.

9. C
Brittany's mark is the highest.

According to condition 1, the order is:

Emily
Peter
Brad

With condition 2,

Emily
Peter
Brad
Brittany

With condition 3,

Emily
Peter
Andrew
Brad
Brittany

The list is from lowest at the top to highest at the bottom, so Brittany's mark is the highest.

10. C
Linda appears in the first and third sentence and so do 'Z' and 'W,' so it must be one of the two. 'Z' is in the same position as Linda in the first sentence and can be eliminated, so Linda must be 'W.'

11. D
'Like' is in all three sentences, so it must be 'B,' 'O' or 'V.' The only one of these three to appear in the third sentence is 'V,' so it must be 'like.'

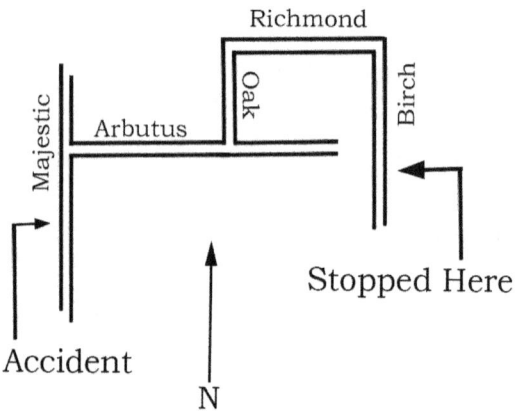

12. C
The vehicle was traveling east on Arbutus.

13. C
The vehicle was traveling east on Richmond.

14. A
C, D, A, B is the correct sequence.

> c. Dispatch reports a beach party
>
> d. You approach a group of teens
>
> a. Teens refuse to give their names
>
> b. Several teens flee the scene

15. D
B, D, C, A is the correct sequence.

> b. A suspect gives his name as Andrew Jones and is released.
>
> d. A records check reveals a person fitting his description is actually Robert Smith with a lengthy list of priors.
>
> c. The suspect is later arrested by other officers.
> a. Robert Smith is charged.

Practice Test Questions Set 2

The questions below are not the same as you will find on the APCAT - that would be too easy! And nobody knows what the questions will be and they change all the time. Below are general questions that cover the same subject areas as the APCAT. So the format and exact wording of the questions may differ slightly, and change from year to year, if you can answer the questions below, you will have no problem with the APCAT.

For the best results, take these Practice Test Questions as if it were the real exam. Set aside time when you will not be disturbed, and a location that is quiet and free of distractions. Read the instructions carefully, read each question carefully, and answer to the best of your ability.
Use the bubble answer sheets provided. When you have completed the Practice Questions, check your answer against the Answer Key and read the explanation provided.

Do not attempt more than one set of practice test questions in one day. After completing the first practice test, wait two or three days before attempting the second set of questions.

Observation – 7 Questions

Professional Judgment: 10 Questions

Recognition/Identification – 3 Questions

ACT – 20 questions

Mathematics - 20 questions

Logic – 20 questions

Observation

	A	B	C	D
1	○	○	○	○
2	○	○	○	○
3	○	○	○	○
4	○	○	○	○
5	○	○	○	○
6	○	○	○	○
7	○	○	○	○

JUDGMENT AND RECOGNITION

	A	B	C	D
1	○	○	○	○
2	○	○	○	○
3	○	○	○	○
4	○	○	○	○
5	○	○	○	○
6	○	○	○	○
7	○	○	○	○
8	○	○	○	○
9	○	○	○	○
10	○	○	○	○
11	○	○	○	○
12	○	○	○	○
13	○	○	○	○

ACT

	A	B	C	D
1	○	○	○	○
2	○	○	○	○
3	○	○	○	○
4	○	○	○	○
5	○	○	○	○
6	○	○	○	○
7	○	○	○	○
8	○	○	○	○
9	○	○	○	○
10	○	○	○	○
11	○	○	○	○
12	○	○	○	○
13	○	○	○	○
14	○	○	○	○
15	○	○	○	○
16	○	○	○	○
17	○	○	○	○
18	○	○	○	○
19	○	○	○	○
20	○	○	○	○

MATHEMATICS

	A	B	C	D
1	○	○	○	○
2	○	○	○	○
3	○	○	○	○
4	○	○	○	○
5	○	○	○	○
6	○	○	○	○
7	○	○	○	○
8	○	○	○	○
9	○	○	○	○
10	○	○	○	○
11	○	○	○	○
12	○	○	○	○
13	○	○	○	○
14	○	○	○	○
15	○	○	○	○
16	○	○	○	○
17	○	○	○	○
18	○	○	○	○
19	○	○	○	○
20	○	○	○	○

Logic

	A	B	C	D
1	○	○	○	○
2	○	○	○	○
3	○	○	○	○
4	○	○	○	○
5	○	○	○	○
6	○	○	○	○
7	○	○	○	○
8	○	○	○	○
9	○	○	○	○
10	○	○	○	○
11	○	○	○	○
12	○	○	○	○
13	○	○	○	○
14	○	○	○	○
15	○	○	○	○
16	○	○	○	○
17	○	○	○	○
18	○	○	○	○
19	○	○	○	○
20	○	○	○	○

Professional Judgment

Scenario: You are called to a robbery and see two cars leaving the scene at high speed. You give chase, however, the cars are driving at very high speed and driving very dangerously.

1. What should you do?

    a. Call dispatch with as much information as possible

    b. Follow the cars and match their speed.

    c. Follow the cars at a high but safe speed, even if you fall behind

    d. Follow the cars but do not exceed the speed limit.

Scenario: You are in a meeting with several colleagues from a neighboring municipality, discussing the events of last night. A radio call comes in reporting an officer needing assistance. The location is very close to your station.

2. What should you do?

    a. Continue with the meeting as others officers will respond.

    b. Leave the meeting immediately and respond to the call

    c. Invite the other officers to respond to the call with you

    d. Wrap up the meeting early and respond to the call

Scenario: You attend a noise complaint and are questioning several teenagers. They have numerous chocolate bars in their pockets and there are chocolate bar wrappers on the ground around them. The teenagers refuse to speak with you unless you arrest them.

3. What should you do?

    a. Call the station and ask if there has been any thefts nearby

    b. Arrest the teenagers

    c. Demand that they provide you with their names

    d. Accuse them of stealing the chocolate bars

Scenario: You are on your lunch break in a local restaurant with your partner. A person approaches you in a panic saying there is a man having a heart attack in the next building.

4. What should you do?

    a. Politely tell the person you are having lunch but will radio in the call.

    b. Leave lunch immediately and investigate the report

    c. Finish you lunch and tell your junior partner to attend to the complaint

    d. Ignore the complaint

Scenario: You apprehend a black suspect apparently leaving the scene of a break and enter. The suspect accuses you of racial profiling.

5. What should you do?

  a. Release the suspect to avoid an ugly scene

  b. Deny the accusation and continue

  c. Explain that you have found him apparently leaving the scene of a crime and would like to ask some questions

  d. Explain the police policy on racial profiling

The black suspect still insists that you are stopping his because of his race and refuses to answer any questions.

What should you do?

  a. You have already explained that you have found him at the scene of a break and enter, and would like to ask some questions. The next step is to explain that if he continues to refuse, you will have to take him to the station for questioning.

  b. Arrest him immediately

  c. Explain the situation again

  d. Avoid an ugly scene and allow him to go

Scenario: You are patrolling a local street and find a couple having a heated argument.

7. What should you do?

  a. Tell the couple to stop arguing

  b. Ask if everything is OK

  c. Listen to the argument and try to resolve

  d. Listen to the argument and take the side of the best argument

Recognition and Identification

8. Choose the person that matches the suspect below.

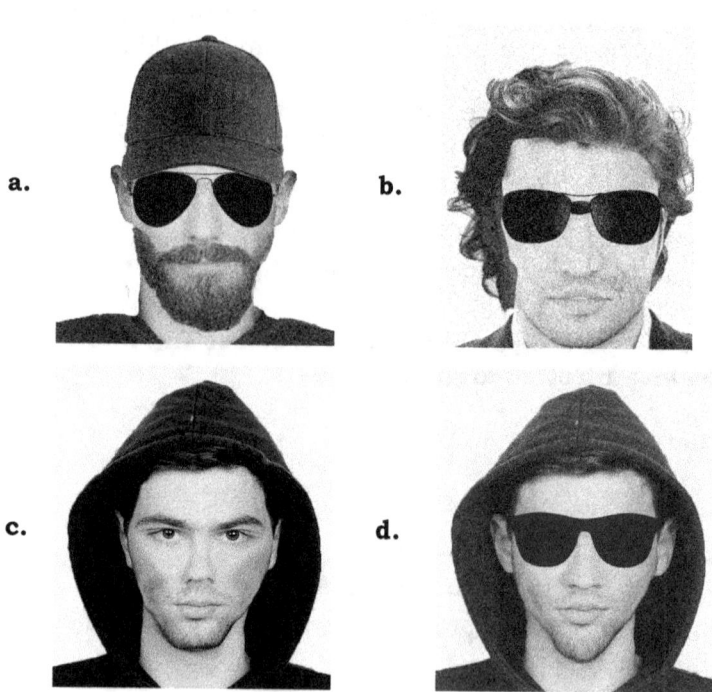

a.

b.

c.

d.

9. Choose the person that matches the suspect below.

a.

b.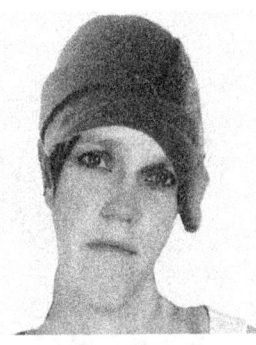

c.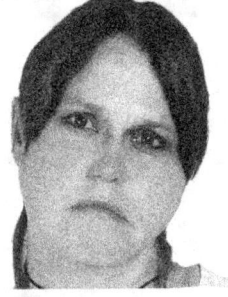

d.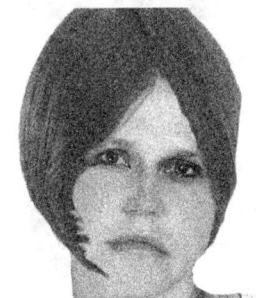

10. Choose the person that matches the suspect below.

a. 　　b.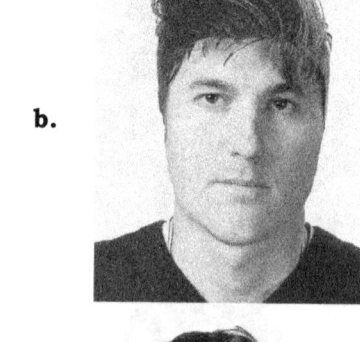

c. 　　d.

Alberta Police Communications Test

1. Choose the best definition of anecdote.

    a. A short account of an incident
    b. Something that comes before
    c. The use of humor, irony, exaggeration, or ridicule
    d. Constant fluctuations

2. Choose the adjective that means shocking, terrible or wicked.

    a. Pleasantries
    b. Heinous
    c. Shrewd
    d. Provincial

3. Choose the noun that means a person or thing that tells or announces the coming of someone or something.

    a. Harbinger
    b. Evasion
    c. Bleak
    d. Craven

4. Choose a word that means the same as the underlined word.

He wasn't especially generous. All the servings were very judicious.

    a. Abundant
    b. Careful
    c. Extravagant
    d. Careless

5. Fill in the blank.

Because of the growing use of _____ as a fuel, corn production has greatly increased.

    a. Alcohol
    b. Ethanol
    c. Natural gas
    d. Oil

6. Fill in the blank.

In heavily industrialized areas, the pollution of the air causes many to develop _____ diseases.

    a. Respiratory
    b. Cardiac
    c. Alimentary
    d. Circulatory

7. Choose the best definition of inherent.

    a. To receive money in a will
    b. An essential part of
    c. To receive money from a will
    d. None of the above

8. Choose the best definition of vapid.

    a. adj. tasteless or bland
    b. v. To inflict, as a revenge or punishment
    c. v. to convert into gas
    d. v. to go up in smoke

9. Choose the best definition of waif.

   a. n. a sick and hungry child
   b. n. an orphan staying in a foster home
   c. n. homeless child or stray
   d. n. a type of French bread eaten with cheese

10. Choose the adjective that means similar or identical.

   a. Soluble
   b. Assembly
   c. Conclave
   d. Homologous

11. Choose the correct spelling.

   a. Correspondence
   b. Corespodence
   c. Correspodence
   d. Correspomdence

12. Choose the correct spelling.

   a. Henmorrhage
   b. Hemmorrhage
   c. Hemorrhage
   d. Hemorhage

13. Choose the correct spelling.

   a. Enviromnment
   b. Environment
   c. Environiment
   d. Enviromment

14. Choose the correct spelling.

    a. Govermment

    b. Goverment

    c. Govenment

    d. Government

15. Choose the correct spelling.

    a. Conceeve

    b. Concieve

    c. Conceive

    d. Conceve

16. Choose the correct spelling.

    a. Describe

    b. Decribe

    c. Decsribe

    d. Discribe

17. Choose the correct spelling.

    a. Liqour

    b. Liquor

    c. Liquer

    d. Liquour

18. Choose the correct spelling.

    a. Succesful

    b. Sucessful

    c. Sucessfull

    d. Successful

19. Choose the correct spelling.

a. Huricane

b. Hurricane

c. Huricane

d. Hurriccane

20. Choose the correct spelling.

a. Precede

b. Preccede

c. Precceed

d. Preceed

21. Choose the sentence below with the correct punctuation.

a. There are many species of owls, the Great-Horned Owl, the Snowy Owl, and the Western Screech Owl, and the Barn Owl.

b. There are many species of owls, the Great-Horned Owl: the Snowy Owl: and the Western Screech Owl, and the Barn Owl.

c. There are many species of owls: the Great-Horned Owl, the Snowy Owl, and the Western Screech Owl, and the Barn Owl.

d. There are many species of owls: the Great-Horned Owl, the Snowy Owl, and the Western Screech Owl, and the Barn Owl.

22. Choose the sentence below with the correct punctuation.

a. In his most famous speech, Reverend King proclaimed: "I have a dream!"

b. In his most famous speech, Reverend King proclaimed; "I have a dream!"

c. In his most famous speech, Reverend King proclaimed. "I have a dream!"

d. In his most famous speech: Reverend King proclaimed, "I have a dream!"

23. Choose the sentence below with the correct punctuation.

a. Puzzled — Joe said, "You aren't going to pay me until ?"

b. Puzzled, Joe said, "You aren't going to pay me until ?"

c. Puzzled, Joe said, "You aren't going to pay me until —?"

d. Puzzled, Joe said, "You aren't going to pay me until, ?"

24. Choose the sentence with the correct usage.

a. Vegetables are a healthy food; eating them can make you more healthful.

b. Vegetables are a healthful food; eating them can make you more healthful.

c. Vegetables are a healthy food; eating them can make you more healthy.

d. Vegetables are a healthful food; eating them can make you more healthy.

25. Choose the sentence with the correct usage.

a. When James went into his room, he found that his clothes had been put in the closet.

b. When James went in his room, he found that his clothes had been put in the closet.

c. When James went into his room, he found that his clothes had been put into the closet.

d. When James went in his room, he found that his clothes had been put into the closet.

26. Choose the sentence with the correct usage.

a. After you lay the books on the counter, you may lay down for a nap.

b. After you lie the books on the counter, you may lay down for a nap.

c. After you lay the books on the counter, you may lie down for a nap.

d. After you lay the books on the counter, you may lay down for a nap.

27. Choose the sentence with the correct usage.

a. He did not have to loose the race; if only his shoes weren't so lose!

b. He did not have to lose the race; if only his shoes weren't so loose!

c. He did not have to loose the race; if only his shoes weren't so lose!

d. He did not have to lose the race; if only his shoes weren't so lose!

28. Choose the sentence with the correct usage.

a. The attorney did not want to prosecute the defendant; his goal was to prosecute the guilty party.

b. The attorney did not want to persecute the defendant; his goal was to persecute the guilty party.

c. The attorney did not want to prosecute the defendant; his goal was to persecute the guilty party.

d. The attorney did not want to persecute the defendant; his goal was to prosecute the guilty party.

29. Choose the sentence with the correct usage.

a. The speeches must precede the election; the election cannot proceed without hearing from the candidates.

b. The speeches must precede the election; the election cannot precede without hearing from the candidates.

c. The speeches must proceed the election; the election cannot precede without hearing from the candidates.

d. The speeches must proceed the election; the election cannot proceed without hearing from the candidates.

30. Choose the sentence with the correct usage.

a. Before a lawyer can rise an objection, he must first rise to his feet.

b. Before a lawyer can raise an objection, he must first raise to his feet.

c. Before a lawyer can raise an objection, he must first rise to his feet.

d. Before a lawyer can rise an objection, he must first raise to his feet.

Mathematics

1. Estimate 2009 x 108.

    a. 110,000
    b. 2,0000
    c. 21,000
    d. 210,000

2. Richard sold 12 shirts for total revenue of $336 at 8% profit. What is the purchase price of each shirt?

    a. $25.76
    b. $24.50
    c. $23.75
    d. $22.50

3. Calculate (3a + 4b) * d when A = 2, b = 4 and d = 8

    a. 40
    b. 150
    c. 112
    d. 176

4. c = 4, n = 5 and x = 3. Calculate 2cnx/2n

    a. 12
    b. 50
    c. 8
    d. 21

5. If a = 12 and b = 8, solve 6b - a + 2a

   a. 12/9
   b. 18
   c. 16
   d. 12

6. Solve √121

   a. 11
   b. 12
   c. 21
   d. None of the above

7. In a local election at polling station A, 945 voters cast their vote out of 1270 registered voters. At polling station B, 860 cast their vote out of 1050 registered voters and at station C, 1210 cast their vote out of 1440 registered voters. What was the total turnout including all three polling stations?

   a. 70%
   b. 74%
   c. 76%
   d. 80%

8. In a factory, the average salary of all employees is $125. The average salary of 10 managers is $300 and average salary of workers is $100. What is the total number of employees?

   a. 30
   b. 40
   c. 25
   d. 50

9. In a 30 minute test there are 40 problems. A student solved 28 problems in first 25 minutes. How many seconds should she give to each of the remaining problems?

   a. 20 seconds
   b. 23 seconds
   c. 25 seconds
   d. 27 seconds

10. The total expense of building a fence around a square-shaped field is $2000 at a rate of $5 per meter. What is the length of one side?

    a. 80 meters
    b. 100 meters
    c. 40 meters
    d. 320 meters

11. In a class of 83 students, 72 are present. What percent of student is absent? Provide answer up to two significant digits.

    a. 12
    b. 13
    c. 14
    d. 15

12. If Lynn can type a page in p minutes, what portion of the page can she do in 5 minutes?

    a. p/5
    b. p − 5
    c. p + 5
    d. 5/p

13. A worker's weekly salary was increased by 30%. If his new salary is $150, what was his old salary?

    a. $120.00
    b. $99.15
    c. $109.00
    d. $115.40

14. Brad has agreed to buy everyone a Coke. Each drink costs $1.89, and there are 5 friends. Estimate Brad's cost.

    a. $7
    b. $8
    c. $10
    d. $12

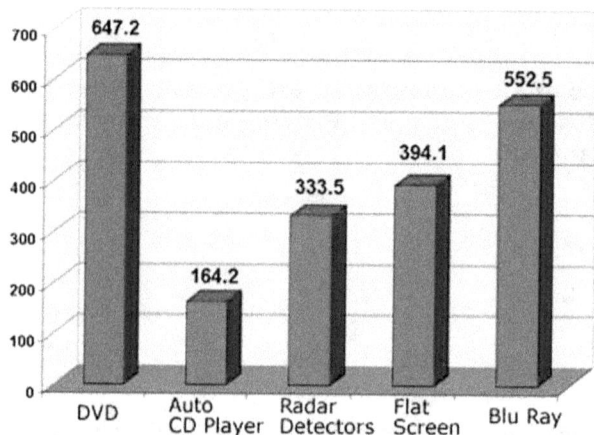

15. Consider the graph above. What is the third best-selling product?

    a. Radar Detectors
    b. Flat Screen TV
    c. Blu Ray
    d. Auto CD Players

16. Which two products are the closest in the number of sales?

    a. Blu Ray and Flat Screen TV
    b. Flat Screen TV and Radar Detectors
    c. Radar Detectors and Auto CD Players
    d. DVD players and Blu Ray

17. Great Britain has a Value Added Tax of 15%. A shop sells a camera for $545. If the VAT is included in the price, what is the actual cost of the camera?

    a. $490.40
    b. $473.91
    c. $505.00
    d. $503.15

18. The owner of a pet store decided to increase the cost of all reptiles 45%. If the initial cost of a reptile was $220, what is the new cost?

    a. $230
    b. $300
    c. $319
    d. $245

19. 5 men have to share a load weighing 10kg 550g equally among themselves. How much will each man have to carry?

    a. 900 g
    b. 1.5 kg
    c. 3 kg
    d. 2 kg 110 g

20. Peter drives 4 blocks to school and back every day. How many blocks does he drive in 5 days?

   a. 20
   b. 30
   c. 40
   d. 50

Logic

1. Consider the following sequence: 3, 5, 10, 12, 24, ... What 2 numbers should come next?

   a. 48, 58
   b. 26, 28
   c. 48, 50
   d. 26, 52

2. Consider the following sequence: 1000, 992, 984, 976, ... What 2 numbers should come next?

   a. 968, 961
   b. 967, 960
   c. 968, 960
   d. 970, 964

3. Consider the following sequence: 0.1, 0.3, 0.9, 2.7, ... What 2 numbers should come next?

   a. -8.1, -24.3
   b. 8.1, 24.3
   c. 5.4, 10.8
   d. -5.4, -10.8

4. Consider the following sequence: 32, 16, 8, 4, ... What 3 numbers should come next?

    a. 2, 1, 0.5
    b. 2, 0, -2
    c. 0, -4, -8
    d. 2, 1, 0

5. Jane spends her free time reading. She likes to read books, magazines, and even newspapers. She reads stories about adventures and fairy tales.

    a. Jane likes to watch television.
    b. Jane spends her free time writing stories.
    c. Jane's hobby is reading.
    d. Jane reads stories in school.

6. The body is made up of many bones. The skull protects the head. The ribs protect the chest. There are also small bones that protect the ears.

    a. Bones are connected to the muscles.
    b. Bones are present in the stomach.
    c. Animals have bones.
    d. Bones protect different parts of the body.

7. Trees give off oxygen. They also provide shade during sunny days. Some trees bear fruits while others are used to build houses.

    a. Trees have many purposes.
    b. Trees aren't important to men.
    c. Birds build nests in trees.
    d. Roots and trunk are parts of a tree.

8. At a liquor store, five cases of beer are stacked. There are five different types, including, Coors, Budweiser, Heineken, Molsons and Carling Lager.

    1. The Coors is higher than the Carling Lager.

    2. There are two cases between the Carling Lager and Heineken cases.

    3. The Budweiser case is third from the top.

If the bottom case is Carling Lager, which case is on top?

    a. Molsons

    b. Coors

    c. Heineken

    d. Either Molsons or Coors

Instructions for questions 9 and 10.

1. each letter always represents the same word.
2. each word is represented by one letter.
3. the letters are not necessarily in the same order as the words.

    M O R T W means

    Peter loves to text Brittany

    M N X T R means

    Susan loves to text Mark

    Q M X R T means

    Andrea loves to text Susan

    M Z R O Y means

    Gabriel wants to email Peter.

9. What letter is "Andrea?"

   a. R
   b. M
   c. Q
   d. Cannot be determined

10. What word is "Z?"

   a. Text
   b. Susan
   c. Gabriel
   d. Cannot be determined.

Scenario: You attend a break and enter and see the suspect leaving the house on Granite St., and runs north. He then turns left on San Pedro, and left on Birch. He cuts through a property on Birch and exits on Richmond. You see him taking the shortcut and continue on San Pedro, turn left on Richmond, and apprehend the suspect on Richmond as he exits the property.

11. What direction was the suspect traveling on San Pedro?

   a. North
   b. South
   c. East
   d. West

12. What direction was the suspect traveling on Birch?

   a. North
   b. South
   c. East
   d. West

13. When you turned left on Richmond, what direction were you traveling?

   a. North
   b. South
   c. East
   d. West

14. Put the statements below into the most logical sequence.

1. A woman calls the station complaining about harassment by her ex husband.
2. You receive the call from dispatch.
3. An officer takes the woman's statement.
4. You question the ex husband.
5. A judge issues a restraining order prohibiting the ex husband from contacting the woman.

   a. 1, 2, 3, 4, 5
   b. 1, 3, 2, 4, 5
   c. 2, 3, 5, 1, 4
   d. 2, 1, 3, 5, 4

15. Put the statements below into the most logical sequence.

1. You ticket one driver for dangerous driving
2. You interview both drivers separately.
3. 2 vehicles collide in the middle of an intersection
4. A vehicles runs a red light.
5. You interview pedestrians on the scene

   a. 1, 2, 3, 4, 5
   b. 1, 3, 2, 4, 5
   c. 2, 3, 5, 1, 4
   d. 4, 3, 2, 5, 1

Answer Key

Professional Judgment

1. C
One of your responsibilities is the safety, which includes yourself. In addition, a high speed chase could endanger innocent people. The best course of action is to follow the cars at a high but safe speed and update dispatch with a description of the cars and any other information you have.

2. B
A primary responsibility is to your fellow officers and this is much more important than your meeting.

3. A
The best course of action is the gather more information and then proceed from there.

4. B
Protection of life is a primary responsibility of a police officer so the best course of action is to investigate the complaint immediately. You can finish lunch later.

5. C
Handling the situation carefully and calmly is important. Stay calm and do not engage. Explain that you have found him apparently leaving the scene of a crime and would like to ask some questions

6. A
While it is important to handle the situation carefully, you have already warned him once and explained the situation. Staying calm, the best course of action is to explain that if he continues to refuse, you will have to take him to the station for questioning

7. B
The best course of action is to ask if everything is OK. No crime is being committed, and no one is being injured.

OBSERVATION

11. B
Janet Benoit is wanted for child neglect.

12. C
Jeffrey Crisp is wanted for sexual assault.

13. C
The Volkswagen Phaeton is from Ontario.

14. D
Nathan Abraham is wanted for domestic assault.

15. A
The modified Chevrolet truck is from the Yukon.

ALBERTA POLICE COMMUNICATIONS TEST

1. A
Anecdote: n. A short account of an incident

2. B
Heinous: adj. shocking, terrible or wicked.

3. A
Harbinger: n. a person of thing that tells or announces the coming of someone or something

4. B
Judicious: Having, or characterized by, good judgment or sound thinking. Careful.

5. B
Ethanol: n. a colorless volatile flammable liquid C_2H_6O.

6. A
Respiratory: adj. Of, relating to, or affecting respiration or the organs of respiration.

7. B
Inherent: Naturally a part or consequence of something.

8. A
Vapid: adj. tasteless or bland.

9. C
Waif: n. homeless child or stray.

10. D
Homologous: adj. similar or identical.

11. A
Correspondence is the correct spelling.

12. C
Hemorrhage is the correct spelling.

13. B
Environment is the correct spelling.

14. D
Government is the correct spelling.

15. C
Conceive is the correct spelling.

16. A
Describe is the correct spelling.

17. B
Liquor is the correct spelling.

18. D
Successful is the correct spelling.

19. B
Hurricane is the correct spelling.

20. A
Precede is the correct spelling.

21. D
A colon informs the reader that what follows the mark proves, explains, or lists elements of what preceded the mark.

22. D
A colon informs the reader that what follows the mark proves, explains, or lists elements of what preceded the mark.

23. C
The dash is used when the speaker cannot continue.

24. D
Healthful vs. Healthy. Use 'Healthy' to describe something that is of good for your health and 'healthful' refers to habits or types.

25. A
In vs. Into. 'In' a room means inside. 'Into' refers to movement or action.

26. C
Lay vs. Lie. 'Lie' requires an object and 'lay' does not. So you can lie down, (no object. and you lay a book on the floor.

27. B
Lose vs. Loose. 'Lose' is to no longer have, or to lose a race. 'Loose' is not tied or able to move freely.

28. D
Persecute vs. Prosecute. To prosecute is to have a legal claim against someone and to persecute is to harass.

29. A
Precede vs. Proceed. To precede, is to go first or in front of. To proceed is to go forward.

30. C
Rise vs. Raise. 'Rise' does not require an object and raise does require an object. You have to 'raise' something.

MATHEMATICS

1. D
2009 X 108 is about 210,000. The actual number is 216,972.

2. A
The price of 12 shirts with profit is 8% = 0.92 X 336 = $309.12 The purchase price of each shirt = 309.12/12 = $25.76

3. D
Substitute the known variables, (3 x 2) + (4 x 4) x 8 =, 6 + 16 x 8, 24 x 8 = 176

4. A
2cnx = 2(4 x 5 x 3)/(2 X 5) =, 2 x 60/2 x 5 =, 120/10 = 12

5. D
Substitute with known variables, (6 x 8) – 12 + (2 x 12) =, 48 – 12 + 24, do the additions first, 48 – (12 + 24) =, 48 – 36 = 12

6. A
$\sqrt{121}$ = 11

7. D
To find the total turnout in all three polling stations, we need to proportion the number of voters to the number of all registered voters.
Number of total voters = 945 + 860 + 1210 = 3015

Number of total registered voters
= 1270 + 1050 + 1440 = 3760
Percentage turnout over all three polling stations
= 3015 * 100/3760 = 80.19%

Checking the answers, we round 80.19 to the nearest whole number: 80%

8. B
Assume the total numbers of employees is x. The total salary of all employees will be 125x. The total salary of the managers = 10 X 300 = $3000. The number of employees = X - 10, so the total salary of employees will be 100 X (X-10).

The equation becomes 100(X - 10) + 3000 = 125X. x = 40.

9. C
The number of remaining questions is 40 - 28 = 12
The time remaining is 30 - 25 = 5 minutes = 5 X 60 = 300 seconds. So the time remaining for each question is 300/12 = 25 seconds.

10. B
Total expense is $2000 and we are informed that $5 is spent per meter. Combining these two information, we know that the total length of the fence is 2000/5 = 400 meters.

The fence is built around a square-shaped field. If one side of the square is "a," the perimeter of the square is "4a." Here, the perimeter is equal to 400 meters. So,

400 = 4a

100 = a → this means that one side of the square is equal to 100 meters.

11. B
If 72 students are present, then 83 - 72 = 11 students are absent. To calculate the percent, the equation will be,

11/83 = x/100
83x = 1100
x = 1100/83
x = 13.25   rounding off - 13% of the students are absent.

12. D
This is a simple direct proportion problem:
If Lynn can type 1 page in p minutes, then she can type x pages in 5 minutes

Cross multiply: x * p = 5 * 1

Then,
x = 5/p

13. D
Let old salary = X, therefore $150 = x + 0.30x$, $150 = 1x + 0.30x$, $150 = 1.30x$, $x = 150/1.30 = 115.4$

14. C
If there are 5 friends and each drink costs $1.89, we can round up to $2 per drink and estimate the total cost at, 5 X $2 = $10.

The actual, cost is 5 X $1.89 = $9.45.

15. B
Flat Screen TVs are the third best-selling product.

16. B
The two products that are closest in the number of sales, are Flat Screen TVs and Radar Detectors.

17. B
Actual cost = X, therefore, $545 = x + 0.15x$, $545 = 1x + 0.15x$, $545 = 1.15x$, $x = 545/1.15 = 473.91$

18. C
Initial cost was $220. New cost = 220 + (45% of 220), 45% of 220, 45/100 x 220 = 99, therefore new price is 220 + 90 = $319

19. D
First convert the unit of measurements to be the same. Since 1000 g = 1 kg, 10 kg = 10 x 1000 = 10,000 + 550 g = 10,550 g. Divide 10,550 by 5 = 10550/5 = 2110 = 2 kg 110 g

20. C
Each round trip will be 8 blocks, so in 5 days, he will drive 5 X 8 = 40 blocks.

Logic

1. D

The sequence is increasing by adding 2 and multiplying 2 alternatively. The next 2 terms are 24 + 2= 26 and 26 x 2 = 52.

2. C

The sequence is decreasing by 8.

3. B

The sequence is increasing by multiplying each the last term by 3. 2.7 x 3= 8.1 and 8.1 x 3 = 24.3

4. A

The sequence is decreasing by dividing the last term by 2.

5. C

The only certain thing is Jane's hobby is reading.

6. D

The only certain thing is bones protect different parts of the body.

7. A

The only certain thing is tree have many purposes.

8. C

Given information is that Carling Lager is on the bottom, and #3 says Budweiser is 3rd from the top. #2 says there are two cases between the Carling Lager and Heineken cases, so the Heineken case must be in position 2.

   1.
   2. Heineken case
   3. Budweiser case
   4.
   5. Carling Lager case

Molsons and Coors are still unknown. #1 says the Coors case is higher than the Carling Lager case, but since we know the Carling Lager case is on the bottom, that doesn't help. Therefore, we cannot determine the positions of the

Molsons or Coors cases.

9. C
"Andrea" is only in sentence 3. Since all three sentences only differ in the names, the corresponding letters found in all three, M R and T must be "loves to text."

"Susan" must correspond to "X," as they both appear in sentences 2 and 3. To find "Andrea," which only appears in sentence 3, look for the only other letter in that sentence, which is Q.

10. D
"M" and "R" appear in all four sentences, so they must be "loves" and "to" which also appear in all four.

The letters "Z" and "Y" only appear in sentence #4. The other difference between sentence #4 are the words "email" and "Gabriel," but we cannot determine which.

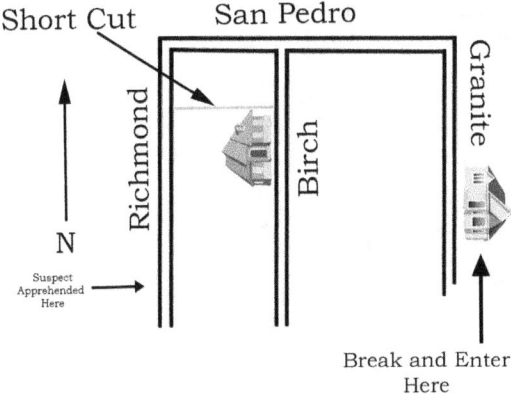

11. D
The suspect was travelling west on San Pedro.

12. B
The suspect was travelling south on Birch.

13. B
You were travelling south when you turned left on Richmond.

14. B
1, 3, 2, 4, 5 is the correct sequence.

1. A woman calls the station complaining about harassment by her ex husband.
3. An officer takes the woman's statement.
2. You receive the call from dispatch.
4. You question the ex husband.
5. A judge issues a restraining order prohibiting the ex husband from contacting the woman.

15. D
4, 3, 2, 5, 1 is the correct sequence.

4. A vehicles runs a red light.
3. 2 vehicles collide in the middle of an intersection
2. You interview both drivers separately.
5. You interview pedestrians on the scene
1. You ticket one driver for dangerous driving

After Taking a Practice Test

What to do after you take a practice test

Go through your answers carefully. For each wrong answer, refer to the explanation, and work through the questions step-by-step.

What kind of question (e.g. reading comprehension, science, algebra, basic math etc.)

Look for patterns in your incorrect answers – what is it exactly that you are doing wrong or don't understand.
What types of questions do you have the most difficulty with? Refer to the tutorials and try to understand the questions.

Getting the Most from Practice Questions

Taking a practice testis probably the best way to prepare for a test.

Quick tips to get the most from practice questions:

Simulate Test Conditions

- Choose a quiet, distraction-free environment.

- Use a timer and allow just under 1 minute per question.

- Avoid using notes or online texts

Take it seriously -

- Treat the practice test as if it's the real exam -

- Familiarize yourself with the format and topics - this will reduce anxiety.

AFTER COMPLETING A PRACTICE TEST

Reviewing your work after you take a practice test is critical.

Immediate Review

- Make a note of any questions you found challenging or topics that felt unfamiliar or difficult.

- How was your time management?

- Overall comfort during the test?

Do a Thorough Review

- Go over your answers focusing on correct and incorrect answers.

- For incorrect answers, identify misunderstandings knowledge gaps or problem subject areas - here is where you need to spend your study time.

Look for Patterns

- Look for recurring themes in your errors to pinpoint specific areas needing improvement.

- Assess whether mistakes were due to content gaps, misinterpretation of questions, or time constraints.

Conclusion

CONGRATULATIONS! You have made it this far because you have applied yourself diligently to practicing for the exam and no doubt improved your potential score considerably! Getting into a good school is a huge step in a journey that might be challenging at times but will be many times more rewarding and fulfilling. That is why being prepared is so important.

Good Luck!

Visit us Online!

WWW.TEST-PREPARATION.CA

ONLINE RESOURCES

How to Prepare for a Test - The Ultimate Guide

https://www.test-preparation.ca/prepare-test/

Learning Styles - The Complete Guide

https://www.test-preparation.ca/learning-style/

Test Anxiety Secrets!

https://www.test-preparation.ca/test-anxiety/

Time Management on a Test

https://www.test-preparation.ca/time-management/

Flash Cards - The Complete Guide

https://www.test-preparation.ca/flash-cards/

Test Preparation Video Series

https://www.test-preparation.ca/test-video/

How to Memorize - The Complete Guide

https://www.test-preparation.ca/memorize/

Online Library of Student Tips and Strategies

https://www.test-preparation.ca/students-say/

www.ingramcontent.com/pod-product-compliance
Lightning Source LLC
Chambersburg PA
CBHW072156070526
44585CB00015B/1175